CONTENTS

INTRODUCTION **5**

PART 1 The Basics of the Computer **6**
The Computer and its Parts **6**
Computer Language **9**

PART 2 The Electronic Card Catalog **10**
OPAC—the Online Public Access Catalog **10**
How to Read a Computerized Card Catalog Entry **11**
Book Entries for OPACs **13**
Reading an OPAC Cookery Printout I **14**
Reading an OPAC Cookery Printout II **15**
OPAC Computer Printout on *Cookery* **16**

Part 3 Computerized Search Strategies **17**
Researching Questions by Subject **17**
Identifying General and Specific Subject Research Questions **18**
Keywords and Search Terms **19**
Finding Keywords and Search Terms **20**
Analyzing a Research Question **21**
Creating Subject Keyword Searches **22**
Database Search Sample I **23**
Database Search Sample II **24**
Keyword Database Searches **25**
Boolean Searches **26**
Conducting Boolean Searches **27**
Truncation Searches **28**
Performing a T. **29**
Creating Multiple **30**

PART 4 CD-ROM Re **31**
Introducing CD-R(. . . .**31**
Choosing a CD-ROM Database **33**
Selecting Sample Science Databases **34**
Choosing Science Databases **35**
Science Database Examples **36**
Selecting Sample History Databases **37**
Choosing History Databases **38**
History Database Examples **39**
Choosing English Databases I **40**

Choosing English Databases II 41
English Database Examples 42
Choosing Mathematics Databases I 43
Choosing Mathematics Databases II .44
Mathematics Database Examples 45
Choosing Fine Arts Databases I 46
Choosing Fine Arts Databases II 47
Fine Arts Database Examples 48
Extended Searches—Stereo Databases 49
Extended Search—Stereo Systems 51

PART 5 Reading Computer Printouts 53
How to Read a Computer Printout 53
Sample Computer Entry 54
Personal Finance—Stock Market Printout I 55
Personal Finance—Stock Market Printout II 56
Computer Printout: Personal Finance—Stock Market 57
Cooking—Entertainment Printout I 61
Cooking—Entertainment Printout II .62
Computer Printout: Cooking—Entertainment 63
Audio Equipment—Automobiles Printout I 67
Audio Equipment—Automobiles Printout II 68
Computer Printout: Audio Equipment—Automobiles 69

PART 6 Citing Electronic Sources 71
MLA and ALA Formats 71
MLA (*Modern Language Association*) Style 72
ALA (*American Library Association*) Style 73

PART 7 Online: The Internet 74
Exploring the Internet 74
How Does the Internet Work? 74
Internet Search Tools 75
Sample Internet Addresses 80
Searching the Internet via Telnet 85
Searching the Internet via Gopher 86
Searching the Internet via the WWW I 87
Searching the Internet via the WWW II 88
Searching Internet Sites 89
Internet News Groups 91
Searching Internet News Groups 92
Searching *Misc.* and *Rec.* Subgroups 93
Identifying *Rec.* Subgroups 94
Internet News *Misc.* and *Rec.* Subgroups 95

Introduction

Today we live in an information age. The world is becoming smaller as we are able to send and receive information faster. That's why computers have become an important part of our world. They enable information to be sent quickly and easily anywhere at any time. This ability to find and receive information via the computer by searching electronic library card catalogs in your school or around the world is truly amazing. *Library Online! A Guide to Computer Research* can help you and your students learn how to use these electronic tools. In it are introductory pages for each topic, student activity pages, and sample information pages, such as a printout of books on the topic of cooking (see p. 16), printouts of book citations (see p. 13), and listings of Internet addresses (see p. 80). In addition to the student activity pages, the sample information pages will also need to be photocopied for students to refer to in completing the related activities. You will of course know your own and your students' knowledge of computers best. Also check with your librarian if you are unsure what computerized resources your library has. Use the student activities in this book as they appear or modify them to suit your class.

Should you start at the beginning of the book? That depends. Do you understand how computers work in processing information? If not, read **Part 1 *The Basics of the Computer*** (see p. 6) to learn some of these computer essentials.

If you know your way around a computer and are ready to assist your students in exploring the electronic library, its resources, and how to find and use them, start at **Part 2 *The Electronic Card Catalog*** (see p. 10). You'll find instructional information followed by reproducible student activity and information pages here.

To expand your computer research to include libraries around the world and online research information and news groups, see **Part 7 *Online: The Internet*** on page 74 for how-to information and reproducible student activity sheets and information pages.

The world of electronic technology is opening up vast new opportunities for learning, gathering, and sharing information. Join in this amazing journey to the *Library Online!*

PART 1

The Basics of the Computer

THE COMPUTER AND ITS PARTS

There are two major types of equipment in PCs, or personal computers: hardware and software. (Note: The term *PC* is used to mean any desktop or laptop computer including IBM-compatibles and Macintoshes.) Hardware is the computer equipment that runs the computer programs. Computer programs or applications are the software. Hardware can include the monitor, CPU or central processing unit (in a desktop computer, the base that the monitor usually sits on), printer, keyboard, mouse, ports, expansion slots, RAM, hard drive, floppy drive, CD-ROM drive, and modem.

OUTSIDE THE COMPUTER: SOME HARDWARE

- **Monitor**—The *monitor* looks like a small TV. It shows on its screen the information processed by the computer. The smallest square on a computer screen is called a *pixel*. Pixels create the picture on a computer screen. Resolution, or the picture's degree of sharpness, is determined by the screen's number of pixels. The letters *VGA* are sometimes listed as part of a computer's description. VGA, or *variable graphics array*, means that your monitor displays images in color.

- **Printer**—The *printer* is the part of the computer that copies what appears on the screen onto paper. There are several types of printers. Dot matrix printers, an older type of printer, use electrical impulses to create images and are commonly found in many libraries. Inkjet printers are newer printers that use tiny dots of ink sprayed onto paper to create better looking images. Laser printers provide the best quality printout. These printers use laser beam technology to print images and, in general, are the most costly.

- **Keyboard**—The computer *keyboard* looks similar to a typing keyboard, but with added features. Extra keys, such as the function keys F1, F2, F3, and so on, provide shortcuts for different commands. These commands can range from printing the information on the computer screen to marking selected pieces of information to quitting a search.

- **Mouse**—In some computers a device called a *mouse* is used to point to an object on the computer screen. You can move the mouse across a mousepad (a small rectangular pad with a special surface) so that the cursor or pointer on the screen moves toward the object that you wish to select. Once the cursor or pointer is positioned where you want it, click the mouse button; this will send a signal to the computer. The results are then seen on the computer screen. Computers without mice move the cursor around by the use of *up*, *down*, *right*, and *left* arrow keys.

INSIDE THE COMPUTER: MAJOR PARTS

- **Ports**—Cables that transmit data to and from a computer plug into *ports* located at the back of most computers. The cables connect a computer's ports to various devices, including modems, printers, and monitors. When information travels through a telephone line, it does so via a *serial port*. A serial port can connect a computer to a printer or a modem. *Parallel ports* work like serial ports, but they can handle much more information. In a similar way, serial printers process information one bit at a time. Parallel printers are like multiline ports that can handle up to eight lines at once.

- **CPU**—The *CPU* or *central processing unit* is the "brains" of the computer. It processes the signals that come into the computer by reading the "address" on the information instructions. It then sends the information on its journey through the computer.

- **RAM, ROM**—A computer has two types of memory: short-term and long-term. *ROM*, or *read-only memory*, is long-term memory. *RAM*, or *random-access memory*, is short-term memory. Information stored in RAM and ROM is measured in *bits* and *bytes*.

- **Bit, Byte**—A *bit*, one unit of computer information, can travel at an incredibly fast rate of speed. Therefore, you cannot see, hear, or feel it. Bits are measured by the digital signals *1* or *0*, where 1=on, 0=off. Eight bits equal one *byte*. Roughly one thousand bytes equal a kilobyte, which is noted as *K*. 1 million bytes, or 1,000K, equal 1 megabyte (MB). One thousand MB equal one gigabyte (GB).

- **Hard Drive**—Your computer reads and stores information on a *hard drive*. The hard drive contains the largest chunk of memory in a computer. Older computers have smaller-sized drives with, for example, 40MB of memory. Newer computers have hard drives ranging in size from 500MB to 2GB of memory. The hard drive controls all the other peripherals, such as the CD-ROM drive, floppy-disk drive, or modem.

PART 1 The Basics of the Computer **7**

- **Floppy Drive and Disks**—Also called a *disk drive*, the internal floppy drive reads and writes information or data files on removable disks. Older disks are 5 1/4" in size and are literally "floppy." Newer disks are smaller (3 1/2") and have a rigid cover that protects the magnetic material inside. Software can be installed onto a computer's hard drive from a disk or a CD-ROM. Disks typically hold about 1.2MB of information which, compared to a CD-ROM, is fairly small.

INSIDE OR OUTSIDE COMPONENTS

- **Modem**—Most computers work on a simple binary system of 0 and 1. (Some use a fuzzy logic system. See p. 9.) The signal to turn on is *1* and the signal to turn off *0*. This is called a *digital* system. Electrical impulses sent in a phone system are *analog* signals. Analog signals transmit sounds or the tones of our voices. The computer cannot communicate in this way though. In order for a computer to talk with a telephone, its digital signals must be converted to analog signals. This is what the *modem* does. Think of it as a translator that changes digital signals to analog signals and vice versa.

- **CD-ROM Drive**—CD-ROMs are read by the computer on a special drive called the *CD-ROM drive*. CD-ROMs look like music CDs, or compact discs, but hold different kinds and amounts of information. Older CD-ROM drives retrieve information at relatively slow rates of speed. Newer drives operate at much faster speeds. A single CD-ROM can hold the information of 200 books, even the information in a 20-volume encyclopedia set!

The Parts of a Computer System

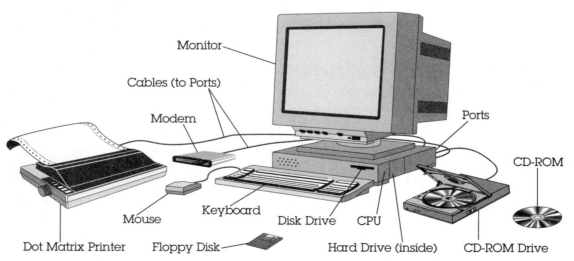

8 PART 1 *The Basics of the Computer*

COMPUTER LANGUAGE

Most computers communicate in the binary language. This type of language expresses information in two ways: "A" or "not A." For instance, *it is this* or *it is not this*. You might like to think of it as a *yes* or *no* way of looking at information, such as "Yes, the grass is green," or "No, the grass is not green." The computer does not store information that the grass is somewhat green.

Computers are being developed that will store information differently than most current computers do. This new way is called *multivalence* or *fuzzy logic thinking*. Binary language is also called *bivalence*. *Multi-* means more than one. So a fuzzy logic computer would have more than one way of handling information.

Fuzzy logic computing is interesting to think about. Several research companies are experimenting with how to improve such information handling. A simple example might be your toaster. If your toaster had the ability to think in "fuzzy" terms, it would work something like this. If the toaster's miniature computer sensed that bread in the toaster was not toasted enough, it would respond by providing more heat. If the bread was toasting nicely, it might decide to stay at its current setting or perhaps slow down the heating process to prevent burning. The toaster programmed with such a computer would not be thinking in terms of "A" or "not A," but in multiple terms.

Understanding how computers "think" will help you in your computerized search for resources and information.

PART 2
The Electronic Card Catalog

OPAC
THE ONLINE PUBLIC ACCESS CATALOG

Most people are familiar with the card catalog in a library. By using the card catalog, any book in a library can be found. Cards representing the title, author, and subject are arranged in alphabetical order. A book can be located easily if you know its title or author or even if you just know the subject of the book.

Today there are computerized tools that can make finding information faster and easier. One of these tools is the *Online Public Access Catalog* or *OPAC*—the computerized library card catalog. Every book is bar coded when it is published. These bar codes look like the bar codes that you see on products in the supermarket. The bar code's series of lines tell the computer basic information about a book. When a book is checked out, a scanner "reads" these lines and converts the coded information into English. That is the information that you can read on the computer screen. Library technicians do their cataloging of books by entering this information into the computer system.

Many, but not all, school and community libraries now have computerized card catalogs. Some libraries are electronically linked with other libraries. Books held by one library may be accessed and borrowed through another community's library. If your library does not yet have a computerized card catalog, you may want to visit a neighboring school or community library that does.

Different cataloging software programs are available for libraries to purchase to create their own computerized card catalogs. Some are similar in how they work and what they show on the monitor screen—others are different. The hardware your library uses will also affect the type of cataloging software used. Suggestions for how to use computerized card catalogs have been kept fairly simple because of these differences. Most libraries provide printed directions with detailed guidelines to help their patrons access the information they are looking for. When in doubt, ask a librarian for assistance. They are always willing to aid you in your search!

© 1997 Good Apple

How to Read
A Computerized Card Catalog Entry

When you check out the card catalog in your library (if it is not automated), you go to one location. Sometimes, you may need to wait if someone else is using the drawer that you need. But if your library has an automated system, there might be more than one computer station or terminal set up to access the OPAC. Since the access time can be fairly quick, you may not have to wait very long to get the information you need. (Note: At times of peak demand or usage, access time can be VERY slow. This happens most often during the daytime hours. Do not be alarmed if the speedy computer terminal you use one day is exceedingly slow the next day. Lots of users, or other people like you, may be looking for information at the same time you are.)

If the library's computer terminal is already turned on, you will probably see a main menu with a list of items to choose from to begin your search. (Note: As there are many different OPAC software systems in use in libraries, be sure to read the specific information and directions that come up on your computer screen and respond to them as prompted.) Among the main menu items will be the computerized card catalog of books and other library holdings. Other holdings could include videos, compact discs, read-alongs, filmstrips, slides, microforms, cassettes, art prints, scores, and maps. Also listed will be a newspaper and magazine index. Sometimes this index contains actual complete articles. If so, this can save you time by allowing you to scan an article to determine its usefulness. Access to the Internet as well as to other electronically connected libraries and their holdings may also be listed in the main menu. These items may appear with headings such as *Internet*, the letters *WWW* (for World Wide Web), or by using the suffix *-net*, as in *COUNTYNET*.

To access the OPAC, most times you would enter the number next to the OPAC listing and then hit the Return or Enter key once. (Note: On occasions when many people are using the system, the computer's response time may be slow. Avoid striking the return key again as this may cause errors and complications.) On the next screen that appears on the computer monitor, you will see a statement or question indicating that information can be accessed by *author*, *title*, *subject*, or *keyword*. To find a work written by the author William Shakespeare, you might type in *A=Shakespeare William* (enter last name first) at the prompt or blinking cursor. For a title search, you might type in *T=Good Apple Homework Helper*. For a search by subject, typing *S=whales* or *S=lions* would turn up resources on whales and lions.

© 1997 Good Apple

PART 2 The Electronic Card Catalog **11**

Some OPACs use the letters *fi* (for "find") followed by *au:*, *ti:*, *su:*, or *k:* and then the *author*, *title*, *subject*, or *keyword* you wish to find. For example, *fi su:cats* will tell the computer to find all books or resources in the card catalog on the subject of cats. (Note: Some OPACs do not distinguish between uppercase and lowercase letters and some do. Check your OPAC's guidelines to be sure you are entering the information correctly.) After you select an access method or field, hit the Enter key once. A list of items in the chosen field will then appear on the screen. To display more information about each book, called a *record* in the computer's database, some OPACs use the command *di*, meaning "display." Another form is *di l* for "display in long form." If you were searching the periodicals database and wished to see a complete article on the computer screen, you may be able to access it by typing in *di l*, as some articles are stored in their entirety in the database. After finding books or other sources to research with, you can print out the results of your computer search. Imagine not having to jot down information before you check the library shelves!

There are many advantages to this kind of system. First, you get fast and accurate information easily. Plus, you get information that you would not get from a manual card catalog system. For example, you can find out from an automated system if a book has been checked out, who checked it out, and when it's due back. All of these features make computerized library service quick, convenient, and enjoyable when you are researching electronically.

Shown on page 13 are two forms of book entries from two different OPAC listings. In the first example, the number at the beginning of the line is the *call number*. The call number tells you how the book is indexed and where it is shelved in the library. For this book the call number is 641.3 HYD. Following the call number are the author's last and first names, the title of the book, the publisher, and the copyright date. The second example shows author, title, and publisher information at the beginning of the record entry. The call number is listed last.

12 **PART 2** *The Electronic Card Catalog*

© 1997 Good Apple

BOOK ENTRIES FOR OPACS

```
Call Number --- Author ----------- Title ----------- Publisher --- © Date
641.3 HYD        Hyde,             What Have You Been      McGraw,         1975
                 Margaret O.       Eating? Do You
                                   Really Know?
```

> **Another form that OPAC systems might use to present information would look something like the following.**

```
Author:              Hull, Gloria T.

Title:               Healing Heart: poems, 1973-1988

Publisher:           Kitchen Table: Women of Color Press, ©1989.

Subjects:            Afro-American women poets.
                     American poetry—20th century.

Library Holdings:

Call Number:         811.54 HUL — Paperback — Available
```

> **In most OPACs, you will be given the option to see more information about the book you've selected. Follow the directions or commands shown on the computer screen to get this detailed information or to start a new or revised search.**

© 1997 Good Apple

PART 2 The Electronic Card Catalog 13

Name _____ Date _____

Reading an OPAC Cookery Printout I

A subject search on *cookery* was conducted, and the results are shown in the sample OPAC printout of available library books, found on page 16. Read the printout to review author, book title, and other information listed. Then, using that information, answer the following questions. Write your answers on the lines provided.

1. Is there a book about microwave cooking? If so, what is its title? _____
_____

2. What book titles are available on African cookery? _____
_____

3. What book titles deal with Japanese cooking? _____
_____

4. Can you find a book about vegetarian cooking? What is its title? _____
_____

5. What is the complete bibliographic information on a book that deals with low-fat cooking? _____
_____

6. How many books were written by Dale Brown? _____

7. What company publishes Dale Brown's books? _____

8. What cookbooks would provide recipes for those watching their weight? _____
_____

© 1997 Good Apple

PART 2 *The Electronic Card Catalog*

Name _____ Date _____

Reading an OPAC Cookery Printout II

Use the sample OPAC printout of library books on the subject of *cookery* (see p. 16) to answer the following questions. Write your answers on the lines provided.

1. What are the copyright dates of Dale Brown's books? _____

2. Who is the author of *Cooking from the Gourmet's Garden*? _____

3. What books could you use to find recipes for Indian food? _____

4. What is the copyright date of the book written by Mary Jane Finsand? _____

5. What countries or regional areas has Jules Bond written about? _____

6. Who are the publishers of Jules Bond's books and when were his books published? _____

7. Who wrote a book on Mexican cooking? _____

8. Are the publishers listed in every *cookery* entry? _____

9. What books would provide recipes for Italian and Scandinavian food? _____

© 1997 Good Apple

PART 2 *The Electronic Card Catalog* 15

OPAC—A COMPUTER PRINTOUT ON "COOKERY"

Call Number	Author	Title	Publisher	Date
641.5 BRO	Brown, Dale.	American Cooking.	Time-Life,	1968.
641.5 BRO	Brown, Dale.	American Cooking: The Northwest.	Time-Life,	1970.
641.5 FIN	Finsand, Mary Jane.	The Complete Diabetic Cookbook.	Sterling,	1990.
641.5 WOL	Wolfe, Robert L. and Diane Wolfe.	Vegetarian Cooking Around the World.	Lerner Publications,	1992.
641.5 BON	Bond, Jules J.	The Chinese Cuisine I Love.	Ameil,	1977.
641.5 BON	Bond, Jules J.	The French Cuisine I Love.	Ameil,	1977.
641.5 BON	Bond, Jules J.	The Mid-Eastern Cuisine I Love.	Ameil,	1977.
641.5 BON	Bond, Jules J.	Recipes from Around the World.	Barron's,	1984.
641.5 CAS	Castle, Coralie.	Cooking from the Gourmet's Garden.	Cole Group,	1994.
641.5 LIN	Linsay, Rae.	The International Party Cookbook.	Drake,	1972.
641.5 LON	Longstreet, Stephen.	The Joys of Jewish Cooking.	Weathervane,	1988. © 1974.
641.4 MAW	Mawson, Monica.	Cooking With Herbs and Spices.	Domus,	1978.
641.5 GAS	Gaspari, Claudia.	Food in Italy.	Rourke Publications,	1989.
641.5 GOM	Gomez, Paolo.	Food in Mexico.	Rourke Publications,	1989.
641.5 NID	Nidetch, Jean.	Weight Watchers New Program Cookbook.	New American,	1978.
641.5 OJA	Ojakangas, Beatrice.	Scandinavian Cooking.	H.P. Books,	1983.
641.5 TSU	Tsuji, Shizuo.	Japanese Cooking.	Kodansha International,	1980.
641.5 VAN	Van Der Post, L.	African Cooking.	Time-Life,	1970.
641.5 KAU	Kaur, Sharon.	Food in India.	Rourke Publications,	1989.
641.5 DOE	Doeser, Linda.	Complete Microwave Cookbook.	International Culinary Society,	1990. © 1989.
641.5 KER	Kerr, Graham.	A Low Fat, Heart Healthy Cookbook.	G.P. Putnam's Sons,	1995.

16 **PART 2** **The Electronic Card Catalog**

© 1997 Good Apple

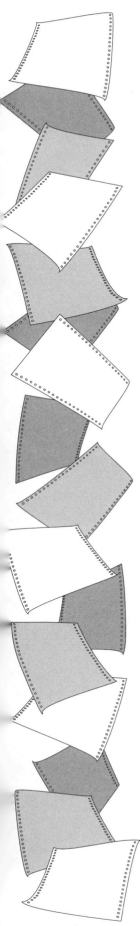

Computerized Search Strategies

PART 3

RESEARCHING QUESTIONS BY SUBJECT

There are many ways to search an OPAC for needed information. If you know the *author* or *title* of a book, you can enter this information and the computer will locate the book or books that fit the search requirements. If you have a *subject* to work with, there are still many search possibilities open to you to help find information. In this section a number of these search options are explored, including subject searches, keyword searches, Boolean searches, truncation searches, and other search variations. One of the most important steps in conducting a computer search, though, is to focus on your research's *subject* or *main idea*. To do that, you need to create a *research question* or *statement*. This query should be as specific as possible. Look at the following sample research question.

> **Where can I find some research information about rain forests?**

Does this question give enough information to begin a computer search with? Not really. Rain forests are a large area about which many different types of information can be found. The question needs to be narrowed so that it is more *specific*. For example:

> **Are rain forests important to our environment?**

In this research question the following terms could be used to begin a computer search: *rain forests, environment,* and *importance of the rain forest*. (Note: You could also start with the broad topic of *rain forests* and then narrow your search to more specific terms as you go. Narrowing your focus at the beginning will save you time and help prevent the slowing down of the library's OPAC database.)

PART 3 Computerized Search Strategies 17

NAME _____   DATE _____

IDENTIFYING GENERAL AND SPECIFIC SUBJECT RESEARCH QUESTIONS

Read the research questions below. Determine if the questions are *general* or *specific*. Circle your answers. On the lines below each question, tell why you think the question is *general* or *specific*.

1. What causes wildlife to be endangered or extinct?   general   specific
   _____
   _____

2. Is endangered wildlife found all over the world?   general   specific
   _____
   _____

3. Is the redheaded woodpecker an endangered species?   general   specific
   _____
   _____

4. How do the rain forests affect our environment?   general   specific
   _____
   _____

5. What is a rain forest?   general   specific
   _____
   _____

18   PART 3 *Computerized Search Strategies*

NAME _____   DATE _____

KEYWORDS AND SEARCH TERMS

Another way to find information about a topic is through *keywords*.
Keywords are those that tell what a research question's main ideas
are. Read the research question below for an example.

Can soil pollution affect water pollution in our environment?

The terms in this question that are keywords are *soil pollution,
water pollution,* and *our environment.*

Read the next research question. What words in it would be good keywords?
Write the keywords on the line provided.

How does the pollution of our waters affect our environment?

_____

Can any of these keywords be combined to create a *searchable term*?
A searchable term is even more specific than a keyword. In this example,
pollution and *water* could become the more usable and narrow search
term *water pollution.*

PART 3 Computerized Search Strategies **19**

NAME _____ DATE _____

FINDING KEYWORDS AND SEARCH TERMS

Find the *keywords* to begin computer searches for the research questions below. Then combine keywords to create narrow *search terms*. Write your answers on the lines provided.

1. What is the major problem of famous sports stars today?

    keywords _____

    search terms _____

2. What do you need to know about packing for a vacation trip?

    keywords _____

    search terms _____

3. What do vitamins have to do with nutrition?

    keywords _____

    search terms _____

4. How do newspapers explain the events of history?

    keywords _____

    search terms _____

5. What do you need to know about caring for a pet?

    keywords _____

    search terms _____

6. How do weather patterns in other parts of the world affect the weather in your area?

    keywords _____

    search terms _____

20   PART 3 *Computerized Search Strategies*

NAME _____ DATE _____

Analyzing a Research Question

Think of an area of interest that you would like to research. Answer the questions below to prepare for your information search. Write your answers on the lines provided.

1. What topic would you like to research?
   _____
   _____

2. What research question could you use to locate information for your topic?
   _____
   _____

3. Analyze your question. Is it *general* or *specific*? If it's *general*, rewrite the question to make it more *specific*.
   _____
   _____
   _____

4. What are the *keywords* for your research question?
   _____
   _____
   _____

5. Can any of the keywords be combined to create narrow *search terms*? Write them here.
   _____
   _____
   _____

PART 3 Computerized Search Strategies **21**

NAME _____   DATE _____

CREATING SUBJECT KEYWORD SEARCHES

Create your own computer searches by subject. Decide on a *research question*, and then identify the general *keywords* and narrow *search terms* for each question. Write your answers on the lines provided below.

1. Research Question #1: _____

   keywords: _____

   search terms: _____

2. Research Question #2: _____

   keywords: _____

   search terms: _____

3. Research Question #3: _____

   keywords: _____

   search terms: _____

4. Research Question #4: _____

   keywords: _____

   search terms: _____

5. Research Question #5: _____

   keywords: _____

   search terms: _____

22 PART 3 Computerized Search Strategies

NAME _____ DATE _____

DATABASE SEARCH SAMPLE I

To help you prepare for your computer search, an additional set of information is provided below. Follow the steps shown identifying the *research question*, *keywords*, and *search terms*. Then note the list of *sample OPAC search terms* to select from. Assuming you wished to find out what the effects of acid rain in North American waters are, choice **(e)** would provide the best place to start a computer database search.

1. **Research Question**
   How does acid rain pollute our bodies of water?

2. **Keywords**
   acid rain, pollution, bodies of water

3. **Search Terms**
   acid rain, water pollution

   (Notice that *bodies of water* was combined with *pollution*. *Pollution* would be too broad and *bodies of water* too vague.)

4. **Sample OPAC Search Terms**
   a. acid rain in rain forests
   b. acid rain in lakes
   c. acid rain in oceans
   d. acid rain in North America
   e. acid rain in North American waters

5. **Best OPAC Search Term to Start a Computer Search With**
   e. *acid rain in North American waters*

PART 3 Computerized Search Strategies **23**

NAME _____   DATE _____

DATABASE SEARCH SAMPLE II

Follow the steps shown below identifying the *research question, keywords, search terms,* and *sample OPAC search terms.* In step **5**, choice **(b)** has been selected as the best place to start a computer database search on this topic. In step **6**, explain why you think this would or would not be the best place to begin this search.

1. **Research Question**
   What causes acid rain pollution?

2. **Keywords**
   acid rain, pollution, causes

3. **Search Terms**
   Acid rain causes, acid rain pollution

4. **Sample OPAC Search Terms**
   a. acid rain—history
   b. acid rain—causes
   c. acid rain—effects
   d. acid rain—water pollution
   e. acid rain—U.S.A.

5. **Best OPAC Search Term to Start a Computer Search With**
   b. *acid rain—causes*

6. Explain why choice (*b*) is or is not a good place to begin searching.

   _____
   _____
   _____
   _____

24   PART 3 *Computerized Search Strategies*

Name _____   Date _____

Keyword Database Searches

Read the research questions below. Identify the questions' *keywords* and *search terms* and write them on the lines provided. Then, review the indexes for each question to find where to begin the computer searches. Circle your answers.

1. *What is important to young people in choosing entertainment?*

    Keywords: _____

    Search terms: _____

    Entertainment Index

    entertainment—books   entertainment—television

    entertainment—movies   entertainment—theater

    entertainment—radio   entertainment—young adult

    entertainment—sports

2. *Does too much television watching affect how young people think?*

    Keywords: _____

    Search terms: _____

    Television Index

    television—history   television—social effects

    television—cable   television—sets, numbers in households

    television—programming

    television—statistics   television—worldwide

PART 3 Computerized Search Strategies   25

NAME _____ DATE _____

Boolean Searches

In addition to the basic subject and keyword searches, you can conduct *Boolean* subject or keyword searches. A Boolean search involves the use of three terms: *and, or, and not.*

Think of these terms as shown in the following diagram.

and	or	and not
A <u>and</u> B	A <u>or</u> B	A <u>and not</u> B

An example of how a Boolean search works is shown below.

> You need to find information about ecology—specifically about the effects of water pollution on ecology outside the United States. Typing the following keywords into the library's computer, using the Boolean terms of *and* and *and not,* would get the information needed.

> **ecology <u>and</u> water pollution <u>and not</u> U.S.A.**

Another example of a Boolean search is this.

> You need information about Martin Luther King, Jr. and the civil rights movement. If you begin your computer search with a simple keyword or author search (*Martin Luther King*) you will get information about many terms related to Martin Luther King. A Boolean search will eliminate information that you do not need. To do that, you would type in the following information.

> **King Martin Luther <u>and</u> civil rights <u>and</u> <u>not</u> the holiday**

(Note: Some OPACs use just the term *not* instead of *and not* in Boolean searches.)

26 PART 3 *Computerized Search Strategies*

NAME _____ DATE _____

Conducting Boolean Searches

Complete *Boolean* searches for the following research questions, using the Boolean terms shown in boldface below. Write your answers on the lines provided.

1. What are the problems of acid rain and the rain forest?

   _____ **or** _____ **and** _____

2. How can you make a pizza at home?

   _____ **and** _____ **and not** _____

3. How do you groom a long-haired dog?

   _____ **and** _____ **and not** _____

4. Where can you find information on battery-operated portable CD players?

   _____ **and** _____ **or** _____

5. What are some of the records set by Olympic athletes in 1996?

   _____ **or** _____ **and** _____

6. What are the names of music groups popular with young people today?

   _____ **and** _____ **or** _____

7. What is the best Internet browser software for Macintosh computers?

   _____ **and** _____ **or** _____

8. What are some of the important battle sites of the Civil War?

   _____ **and** _____ **or** _____

PART 3 Computerized Search Strategies **27**

NAME _____ DATE _____

TRUNCATION SEARCHES

A *truncation* search is another way to do a computer search. To do a truncation search, you truncate, or shorten, your keyword or search term. Suppose that you want several types of information that can be accessed by typing in all the various forms of a search word. Instead of typing each search word, you *truncate* your search term. (Note: a truncation search can be conducted in addition to a Boolean or keyword search.)

For example, if you need information about pollution, you would type **pollu***. Read the results below of a truncation search on this research question.

> *How can we educate our young people about the problems of pollution?*

The shortened form of the word *pollution* is used in this truncation search. (Note: * is the star, or asterisk, on the computer keyboard. Some computers use the question mark: ?)

Pollu*	types of:	
	pollute	waters
		soil
		air
	polluters	offenders
	polluting	agencies that deal with polluters
	pollution	causes
		education
		effects
		government laws
		history

Using the truncation search method yielded many options to choose from for this search.

28 **PART 3 Computerized Search Strategies**

NAME _____ DATE _____

Performing a Truncation Search

Think of an interesting research question and perform a *truncation* search for it. Answer the questions below to complete the search. Write your answers on the lines provided.

1. What is your research question? _____
   _____
   _____
   _____

2. What are the keywords or search terms for your question? _____
   _____
   _____
   _____
   _____

3. What keywords can you *truncate*, or shorten? _____
   _____

4. What other search terms might your search uncover? _____
   _____
   _____
   _____
   _____
   _____
   _____

PART 3 Computerized Search Strategies

NAME _____   DATE _____

Creating Multiple Search Strategies

Create keyword, Boolean, and truncation searches as indicated for each of the research questions below. (Choose two of the following Boolean terms, *and*, *or*, and *and not*, for use in your Boolean search.) Write your answers on the lines provided.

1. Are there any books about pandas and endangered species in China?

    keyword search _____

    _____

    Boolean search _____

    _____

    truncation search _____

    _____

2. What is the difference between sauté and fry cooking?

    Boolean search _____

    _____

    truncation search _____

    _____

3. What was important about Abraham Lincoln's Gettysburg Address?

    keyword search _____

    _____

    Boolean search _____

    _____

30   PART 3 Computerized Search Strategies

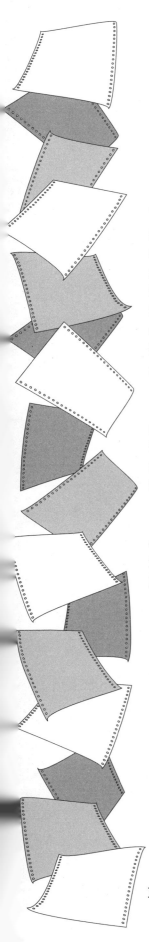

CD-ROM Research Databases

PART 4

INTRODUCING CD-ROM DATABASES

When using your library's computer CD-ROM database resources, you need to know how to select a source for your research. The process of selecting CD-ROMs is very much like the one for print or book source research. Information that is not stored in print form is called nonprint information. Nonprint information is stored on CD-ROMs. The information on these database discs is permanent. It can't be rewritten. (Discs are being developed that can be changed so that information may be updated, added, or deleted as needed. Many companies are now moving into this type of information market.)

Before you can sit down at a computer workstation and pop in a database CD-ROM, you need to know what the CD-ROM information can and cannot do for you. To know what CD-ROM to select, you need to analyze your research questions so that you can search with the CD-ROM that best suits your research needs.

For example, if your research question requires searching in an encyclopedia, you wouldn't go to a CD-ROM that has a dictionary on it. Suppose you are researching acid rain. Which of the following CD-ROM databases might help you?

1. ProQuest—Resource/One (UMI, Ann Arbor, MI)—articles from 130 periodicals

2. SIRS Researcher (SIRS, Boca Raton, FL)—database of physical and social sciences articles from many sources

3. CD NewsBank (NewsBank, Inc., New Canaan, CT)—articles from 100+ newspapers and 8 newswire services

4. McGraw-Hill Multimedia Encyclopedia of Science and Technology (McGraw-Hill Inc., New York, NY)—science encyclopedia

The first database is a list of magazine articles. The second database contains a list of selected articles in the areas of health, science,

PART 4 CD-ROM Research Databases **31**

and the environment. The third database covers a number of U.S. and international newspapers, and the last deals with science encyclopedia-style articles.

Where would you start? A search could be started with the encyclopedia database. This strategy gives an overview of your topic as well as basic information about it. Needed definitions can also be found here. Then, by looking at the SIRS database, more current information could be added.

There are many CD-ROM databases to choose from, and each library's resources will be different. A sample listing of other CD-ROMs that you may find useful is shown below.

- Zak's Look It Up! (Compton's NewMedia, Carlsbad, CA)—encyclopedia, dictionary, thesaurus, atlas, biographies, and articles for children ages 6 to 12

- Compton's Interactive Encyclopedia (Compton's NewMedia, Carlsbad, CA)—multimedia encyclopedia

- World News Digest (Facts on File, New York, NY)—articles and maps on news events from 1980–1995

- Science on File (Facts on File, New York, NY)—encyclopedia with images and drawings

- Landmark Documents in American History (Facts on File, New York, NY)—biographies, speeches, letters, debates, treaties, presidential inaugurals, and more

- Middle Search (EBSCO Publishing, Peabody, MA)—articles and abstracts for middle/junior high school students

- SIRS Discoverer (SIRS, Inc., Boca Raton, FL)—articles and images from 450 magazines, newspapers, and government documents; also an almanac and headline news summaries

- Picture Atlas of the World (National Geographic Society, Washington, DC)

- Mammals: A Multimedia Encyclopedia (National Geographic Society, Washington, DC)

- The Presidents: A Picture History of Our Nation (National Geographic Society, Washington, DC)

32   PART 4 CD-ROM Research Databases

NAME _____   DATE _____

CHOOSING A CD-ROM DATABASE

Review the CD-ROM databases listed below. Select the ones you would use to begin computer searches for each of the following research questions. Write your answers on the lines provided.

CD-ROM Databases
1. ProQuest Resource/One—130 periodicals (magazine articles)
2. SIRS Researcher—social sciences database (health, science, and environmental articles)
3. CD NewsBank—100+ newspapers (U.S. and international)
4. McGraw-Hill Multimedia Encyclopedia of Science and Technology (encyclopedia-style articles)

1. Where did the most recent oil spill take place?
   _____

2. What are the latest treatments available for bone cancer? _____
   _____

3. What is Italy doing about water pollution? _____
   _____

4. What is the future of the electric car? _____
   _____

5. What is the U.S. President's view on recycling? _____
   _____

6. When did Russian and American astronauts first travel in space together? _____
   _____

7. What is the favorite pet of most Americans? _____

PART 4 *CD-ROM Research Databases* **33**

NAME _____   DATE _____

Selecting Sample Science Databases

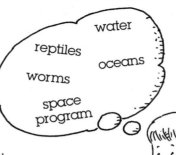

Read the sample science databases listed below. Think about which database you would use to find information for the following research questions. Match up the databases with the questions and write your answers on the lines provided. (Note: The databases listed below are fictitious but your library may have CD-ROM databases with similar information to search.)

Sample Science Databases

Encyclopedia of Reptiles	Oceans of the World
The Environment	World of Invertebrates
Space and Travel	Science: Matter
Movement and Mechanics	Gasses and Light

1. What elements does water consist of? _____
   _____

2. Is a worm an invertebrate? _____
   _____

3. Is the gila monster a reptile? _____

4. Are oceans different from seas? _____

5. What is the basic principle behind the lever? _____
   _____

6. When did the space program begin? _____

7. Is the greenhouse effect getting worse? _____

8. What is the speed of light? _____

34 PART 4 CD-ROM Research Databases

NAME _____   DATE _____

Choosing Science Databases

Review the science database examples found on page 36. Evaluate the research questions below to identify the databases that could be used to begin computer searches. Write your answers on the lines provided. (Note: The databases listed are fictitious but your library may have CD-ROM databases with similar information to search.)

1. Are there endangered wolves in North America? _____
   _____

2. What are weather maps and how are they used? _____
   _____

3. Does Saturn really have rings? _____

4. How does a root grow? _____
   _____

5. What is the difference between a lateral and an apical bud? _____
   _____

6. What do the planets in our galaxy look like? _____
   _____

7. What does the song of the chickadee sound like? _____
   _____

8. What does the Milky Way look like? _____
   _____

9. What is the difference between the red-winged blackbird and the American blackbird?
   _____

PART 4 CD-ROM Research Databases   35

Science Database Examples

Audubon's Birds of America
Provides over 1,600 pages plus 500 color prints and bird call recordings.

Planet Earth and Beyond
Interviews experts who know about the planets.
Includes 250 photographs.

Encyclopedia of U.S. Endangered Species
Reports on 100 U.S. species with list of endangered species.

Earth Science Explorations
Explores geology, meteorology, and astronomy.

Solar System Facts
Covers all planets and their moons plus life on other planets.

Exploring Plant Science
Explains the growth of plants.

The Environment
Explains the problems of water, air, and soil pollution as well as the greenhouse effect.

Animals and Their Classifications
Explains vertebrates and invertebrates, including mammals, fish, reptiles, birds, and insects.

Science: Matter
Reports on atoms, subatomic particles, energy, magnetism, and electricity.

Movement and Mechanics
Covers principles of friction, levers, pulleys, and wheels.

Space and Travel
Discusses the space program.

Name _____   Date _____

Selecting Sample History Databases

Choose sample history databases from the list below to use for researching the following questions. Write your answers on the lines provided. (Note: The databases listed below are fictitious but your library may have CD-ROM databases with similar information to search.)

Sample History Databases		
State Fact Book	U.S. Geography	World Geography
The Elections	History of Asia	World Cultures

1. Is Kentucky close in size to West Virginia? _____
   _____

2. How does a person run for an elected office in the United States? _____
   _____

3. What are the capitals of New York, New Jersey, and Minnesota? _____
   _____

4. What are the customs of China? _____

5. Where can you find a map of the capital of Maine? _____
   _____

6. What states border Arkansas? _____

7. What was the Korean War about? _____
   _____

8. Where is Tibet located? _____

PART 4 CD-ROM Research Databases   37

NAME _____ DATE _____

CHOOSING HISTORY DATABASES

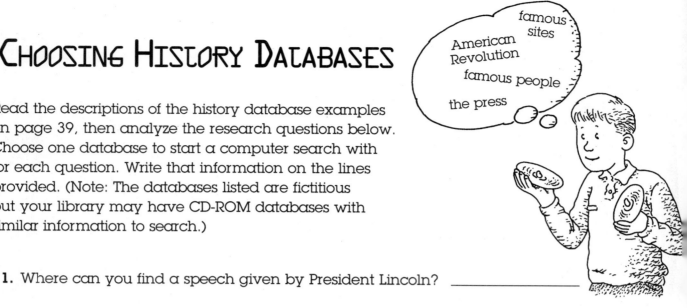

Read the descriptions of the history database examples on page 39, then analyze the research questions below. Choose one database to start a computer search with for each question. Write that information on the lines provided. (Note: The databases listed are fictitious but your library may have CD-ROM databases with similar information to search.)

1. Where can you find a speech given by President Lincoln? _____
   _____

2. Why is Martin Luther King, Jr. a famous American? _____
   _____

3. Is Mt. Rushmore in the national list of famous places? _____

4. Who fired the first shot in the American Revolution? _____
   _____

5. Where can you find a map of Poland? _____
   _____

6. How did the Plains Indians build their homes? _____
   _____

7. Did President Jefferson make a speech when he won the election? _____
   _____

8. Is there a newspaper article on the first American in space? _____
   _____

9. Where can you find a map of the United States? _____
   _____

10. Where can you find information on Malcolm X? _____

History Database Examples

Encyclopedia of the American Indian
Covers tribes, locations, and customs.

Encyclopedia of the American Revolution
Covers the period from colonial times to the end of the revolution.

Atlas of U.S. Presidents
Includes biographies as well as speeches of all U.S. presidents.

World History Fact Book
Covers world history and includes maps, photographs, and animation.

U.S. History—Story of Our Nation
Reports on historical figures and major events with newspaper coverage.

Black American History
Covers U.S. history and the civil rights movement to the present time.

Famous Places
Covers unusual or famous places throughout the world.

History of Europe
Covers the culture and history of all countries in Europe through 1995.

History and Culture of South America
Covers the culture and history of South American countries.

Presidents
Includes portraits, biographies, election results, maps, essays,
and timelines.

The American Constitution
Explains the origins of the American Constitution. Includes
biographies of historical figures involved in its making.

U.S. Geography
Covers states and their capitals. Many detailed maps included.

The Elections
Explains the process of participating in U.S. elections.

PART 4 CD-ROM Research Databases

NAME _____   DATE _____

Choosing English Databases I

Analyze the research questions listed below. What English databases (see examples on p. 42) would you use to find information for each of the questions? Write your answers on the lines provided. (Note: The databases listed are fictitious but your library may have CD-ROM databases with similar information.)

1. How do you use a comma correctly? _____
   _____

2. What are the primary rules of spelling? _____
   _____

3. What are the basic steps of how to do a research paper? _____
   _____

4. You need help in writing a short story. Where can you get that help? ___
   _____

5. How do you use the punctuation guide in the dictionary? _____
   _____

6. Where can you get help in writing a nonfiction article for the school newspaper?
   _____

7. Is Walt Whitman a famous American poet? _____

8. Is *The Glass Menagerie* an American play? _____
   _____

9. What is the name of a famous British play? _____
   _____

40 PART 4 CD-ROM Research Databases

NAME _____   DATE _____

CHOOSING ENGLISH DATABASES II

Analyze the English database examples found on page 42. What databases would you use to find information for the following research questions? Write your answers below. (Note: The databases listed are fictitious but your library may have CD-ROM databases with similar information to search.)

1. What database will help you with your vocabulary? _____
   _____

2. Is the outline a major part of the research paper? _____
   _____

3. What is the difference between a fact and an opinion? _____
   _____

4. Which is the correct spelling—*color* or *colour*? _____

5. What is the difference between a colon and a comma? _____
   _____

6. How do you pronounce *jaguar*? _____
   _____

7. How do you outline a research paper? _____
   _____

8. What is the origin of the word *history*? _____
   _____

9. What is a definition paragraph? _____
   _____

PART 4 CD-ROM Research Databases **41**

ENGLISH DATABASE EXAMPLES

Reading Readiness
Explains the process of finding main ideas, details, facts or opinions, and drawing conclusions.

The Grammar Game
Explains the rules of grammar and punctuation.

Dictionary Skills
Explains how to use the dictionary.

Writer's Program I
Provides a complete guide to writing nonfiction.

Writer's Program II
Provides a complete guide to writing fiction.

Vocabulary Do!
Provides a practice guide to improve your vocabulary.

Speller's Guide to Success
Explains the rules and practices of spelling.

How to Do Research
Explains the steps in the research process.

Literature of the World
Covers the plays of famous writers.

Modern Poetry
Tells about American poets of modern times.

Drama I
Provides information on European plays of the early nineteenth century.

Essays
Provides information on the essays of the world's thinkers.

Drama II
Tells about American plays from 1870–1970.

© 1997 Good Apple

42 PART 4 *CD-ROM Research Databases*

NAME _____ DATE _____

Choosing Mathematics Databases I

Read each research question below. Choose a mathematics database (see examples on p. 45) to start your research for each of the questions. Write your answers on the lines provided. (Note: The databases listed are fictitious but your library may have CD-ROM databases with similar information to search.)

1. Where can you find a series of problems that involve decimals? _____

2. Where can you locate an article about mathematics and computers? _____

3. The report your group is working on needs to have five charts. What database might help? _____

4. Where can you get information on your favorite pastime—games? _____

5. How can you make a graph for your history class report on the stock market?
_____

6. Is 16 ounces equal to 448 grams? _____

7. Where can you get help solving your baseball team's three math problems?
_____

8. How do you divide compound fractions? _____

NAME _____   DATE _____

Choosing Mathematics Databases II

Find the mathematics databases (see examples on p. 45) that would be good starting places to research the questions listed below. Write your answers on the lines provided. (Note: The databases listed are fictitious but your library may have CD-ROM databases with similar information to search.)

1. What is a bar graph? _____

2. How can you make a mathematical crossword puzzle? _____
   _____

3. Are line, circle, or pie graphs most often used in math problems? _____
   _____

4. How can you use math to get baseball players' batting averages? _____
   _____

5. What database will help you with word problems? _____
   _____

6. What decimal can 1/2 be changed to? _____
   _____

7. Where can you find out how to create a table for your math class? _____
   _____

8. How can you use a computer to help you understand math? _____
   _____

9. Where do you go for help with fractions? _____
   _____

44 PART 4 CD-ROM Research Databases

Mathematics Database Examples

Fractions: Addition, Subtraction, Multiplication, and Division
Explains the four mathematical functions of fractions.

Sports Math
Provides math problems that are connected
to sports situations.

Word Problems
Provides in-depth examples of everyday word problems.
Step-by-step examples.

Weights and Measures
Explains the math that is used in weights
and measures.

Computer Math
Explains math word problems using a computer.

Math Puzzlers
Includes math puzzles and games.

Graphs
Tells how to use math to create graphs.

Using Math to Create Charts
Covers the math basics needed to create charts
and tables.

Decimals
Explains how to use decimals in mathematics.

NAME _____   DATE _____

CHOOSING FINE ARTS DATABASES I

Read the research questions below. Choose the fine arts databases (see examples on p. 48) to use in researching each question. Write your answers on the lines provided. (Note: The databases listed are fictitious but your library may have CD-ROM databases with similar information to search.)

1. Is the bagpipe a native instrument of Scotland? _____

2. How is watercolor painting different from oil painting? _____
   _____

3. Where can you find five American folk songs? _____
   _____

4. What is the difference between the orchestra and the symphony? _____
   _____

5. What should you have in your art studio? _____
   _____

6. What kinds of musical instruments do the Chinese use? _____
   _____

7. How is Irish music different from Indian music? _____
   _____

8. What does the famous painting of the Mona Lisa look like? _____
   _____

9. What database presents songs of native cultures and their writers? _____
   _____

NAME _____   DATE _____

CHOOSING FINE ARTS DATABASES II

Read the research questions below. Choose fine arts databases from the list of examples on page 48 to start your research for each question. Write your answers on the lines provided. (Note: The databases listed are fictitious but your library may have CD-ROM databases with similar information to search.)

1. What instruments are used in jazz? _____
_____

2. What does a music staff look like? _____
_____

3. What are some of the subjects painted by the artist Claude Monet? _____
_____

4. How do you use line in pen and ink drawings? _____
_____

5. Where did Western music come from, and how did it develop? _____
_____

6. Who were some of the world's famous painters in the eighteenth and nineteenth centuries? _____

7. Where can you learn the how-to's of painting in watercolor? _____
_____

8. What elements are considered in creating a piece of art? _____
_____

PART 4 CD-ROM Research Databases 47

FINE ARTS
DATABASE EXAMPLES

Complete Guide to Watercolor Painting
Explains the basic techniques of watercolor painting.

Setting Up a Basic Art Studio
Covers the ins and outs of getting the right materials
for the basic studio.

Complete Guide to Oil Painting
Discusses the basics of beginning oil painting.

Design and Composition in Basic Painting
Explains how to use these elements in creating a painting.

Famous Painters and Their Works
Discusses the major artists of Europe to the present time.

Chinese Ink Painting
Provides a complete course in Chinese ink painting.

Basic Brushstrokes of Ink Painting
Explains style and techniques.

Basic Elements of the Orchestra
Explains how the orchestra works.

Music! Music! Music!
Explores instruments used to create music heard
throughout the world.

History of Western Music
Explores the roots of Western music and its history.

The American Folksong and Its History
Discusses the folksong in America.

History of Oriental Music
Explains the rich culture of Asian music.

Know Your Music
Provides basic musical terms and their meanings.

library.wustl.edu
lynx.cc.ukans.edu
fedix.fie.com
mrcnext.cso.uiuc.edu/pub/etext
ftp.spies.com/library
photo1.si.edu
marvel.loc.gov

© 1997 Good Apple

NAME _____   DATE _____

EXTENDED SEARCHES:
STEREO DATABASES

Sometimes you may have to search further for the information that you
need. Each time a new screen appears on the computer monitor, additional
"see also" references may be given. By selecting these "see also" references,
additional topics related to your subject query can be viewed.

For example, if you are looking for information on how to buy a good
set of headphones for your stereo system, you might type in *stereo systems*
and *headphones* and the following would come up on the screen.

Headphones

Reviews

Sound systems

It's possible that the three topics shown above are just a few of many
available selections. Choose *headphones* by clicking on it or entering its
number. A new screen appears on the monitor with 12 listings under *headphones*. The topics range from *how to analyze headphones* to the *usage of
headphones*.

Headphones

see also   Portable stereos

Analyze

Design and construction

Equipment and supplies

Evaluation

Health aspects

Innovations

Marketing

Product introduction

PART 4 CD-ROM Research Databases 49

Purchasing

Recreational aspects

Safety and security measures

Usage

Under the heading of *headphones* on this screen is a "see also" reference. If you click on or select *(see also) portable stereos,* you will bring up yet another screen with the following additional information.

Portable Stereos

see also Audio cassette players and recorders

    Compact disc players

    Headphones

    Portable radios

    Design and construction

    Equipment and supplies

    Evaluation

    Product introduction

    Purchasing

On this new screen an additional nine topics are displayed. If you are looking for information on how to buy headphones, which topic would you choose? If you don't know much about your subject, you might choose design and construction. You might choose evaluation, product information, or purchasing if you are thinking about buying headphones.

Searching requires the skill of knowing what information you want and how bits of information are related. As you move from computer screen to computer screen, take the time to analyze what you are looking at and how it relates to what you are looking for.

50 *PART 4 CD-ROM Research Databases*

NAME _____ DATE _____

EXTENDED SEARCH: STEREO SYSTEMS

Read the research questions on stereo systems, listed below, then review the sample database information on page 52. For each question, find as many database categories that could be searched to obtain the needed information. Write your answers on the lines provided.

1. Where can you find information on the newest stereo headphones available?

   _____

   _____

2. Where would you search to find information on how to do simple repairs to a CD player? _____

   _____

   _____

3. The headphones to your portable tape player are missing one of the padded ear parts. How do you find a replacement? _____

   _____

4. You've heard that excessive use of stereo headphones can cause hearing damage. Where can you find the latest information on this? _____

   _____

   _____

5. Your portable CD player needs new dry-cell batteries. Where can they be bought?

   _____

   _____

PART 4 CD-ROM Research Databases **51**

COMPUTER PRINTOUT: HEADPHONES—STEREOS

HEADPHONES
    Reviews
    Sound systems

HEADPHONES
see also Portable stereos
      Analyze
      Design and construction
      Equipment and supplies
      Evaluation
      Health aspects
      Innovations
      Marketing
      Product introduction
      Purchasing
      Recreational aspects
      Safety and security measures
      Usage

PORTABLE STEREOS
see also Audio cassette players and recorders
      Compact disc players
      Headphones
      Portable radios
      Design and construction
      Equipment and supplies
      Evaluation
      Product introduction
      Purchasing

© 1997 Good Apple

Reading Computer Printouts

PART 5

How to Read a Computer Printout

Once you have done your computer search and have turned up records listing the books, magazines, periodicals, or other sources containing information on your topic, you must decipher what the records tell you. Reading computer entries is fairly easy. A computer card catalog entry is similar to a printed card catalog form of the same information. It may be arranged in a different way, but the information is the same. What you need to know is *what* information is available to you, *how to use* the information in your search process, and *how to read* this information. The kinds of information that computer printouts can provide are shown below.

- **Title**—The first words will give you the title of the periodical.
- **Authors**—The authors of the article are listed last name first, first name last for easy reading and use.
- **Journal**—This is the title of the periodical. In brackets you'll find the abbreviation for the title.

Under the journal part of the entry you'll find more information. For example,

- **ISSN** is the international standard serial number. This is just another way of keeping track of the periodical.
- **Journal Group**—This bit of information tells you what type of periodical the magazine is a member of. For example: *Education* is the group for a magazine called *Educational Digest*.
- **Vol**—Gives the volume number of the magazine.
- **Issue**—Gives the issue number of the magazine.
- **Date**—Gives the date of the magazine.
- **P**—Gives the page.
- **Type**—Gives the style in which the information is given, such as interview or discussion.
- **Illus**—Tells the number of illustrations in the article.

After the journal information you will find the following.

- **Subjects**—Gives other words under which you can find information.
- **Abstract**—Provides a short summary of the article.

Sample Computer Entry

Title: Computers and Libraries

Authors: Chip, Micro, and Bit, Harvey

Journal: Libraries and School Computers [LSC]   ISSN: 0249-4951

abbreviation for the magazine's name

Journal Group: Education   Vol: 18   Iss: 6

type of magazine   **volume number**   **issue number**

Date: June 1996   p: 6

date of magazine   **page number in the article**

Type: Interview   Length: medium

type of article

Illus: chart

type of illustrations

Subjects: School libraries, computers

subjects under which you might find this entry

Abstract: What to consider when adding computers to a school
                library and computerizing the library's card catalog

article summary

54   PART 5 Reading Computer Printouts

Name _____   Date _____

Personal Finance: Stock Market Printout I

Read the computer printout titled "Personal Finance—Stock Market" on pages 57–60 and use it to answer the following research questions. Include the dates and titles of the periodicals. Write your answers on the lines provided.

1. Who are the authors of the article "Three Stocks for Tomorrow Beat Today's Blue Chips"? _____

2. Who is the author of "32 Investments to Buy—and 9 to Shun—in '92"? _____

3. Who wrote "Bargains in Blue Chips"? _____

4. Who is the author of "Big Returns in Small Packages"? _____

5. Who is the author of "Buying Blue Chips at Bargain Prices"? _____

6. Who is the author of "You Can Rely on Stocks, but Don't Trust Them Blindly"? _____

7. Who wrote the article, "Blue Chips: For Clues to the Economy's Direction, Watch Big Retailers"? _____

PART 5 Reading Computer Printouts **55**

Name _____   Date _____

Personal Finance: Stock Market Printout II

Read the computer printout on pages 57–60. Can you find the articles that would help to answer the following research questions? Write the title and author information for these articles on the lines provided.

1. What title would give you advice on how to balance your investment portfolio? _____
   _____

2. Is there any information on long-term bonds? _____
   _____

3. Can you find any information on stocks of major stores? _____
   _____

4. Is there any relationship between the stock market and the U.S. economy?
   _____

5. Where can you find information on stocks of companies that are laying off employees? _____
   _____

6. Is there any information on what stocks to buy in a slowing economy?
   _____
   _____

7. Clint Willis and Baie Netzer are the authors of what article? What journal is the article found in? _____
   _____

56   PART 5 *Reading Computer Printouts*

COMPUTER PRINTOUT: PERSONAL FINANCE—STOCK MARKET

Record 1

Access No:	00396669 ProQuest Resource/One
Title:	Light-Blue Chips Offer Heavy-Duty Growth
Authors:	Anonymous
Journal:	Money [MON] ISSN: 0149-4953
	Jrnl Group: Business Vol: 18 Iss: 6
	Date: Jun 1989 p: 12 Type: Commentary
	Length: Medium Illus: Table
Subjects:	Investments; Securities
Abstract:	Investments in blue chip stocks are always advised in a slowing economy. Analysts are now advising investors to put their money into so-called "light-blue chips," stocks of mid-sized companies that can turn in consistent gains.

copyright © 1996 by UMI Company. All rights reserved.

Record 2

Access No:	00372472 ProQuest Resource/One
Title:	Big Returns in Small Packages
Authors:	Laderman, Jeffrey M
Journal:	Business Week [Industrial/Technology Edition] [BWE]
	ISSN: 0739-8395 Jrnl Group: Business Iss: 3101
	Date: Apr 17, 1989 p: 74-75 Type: Feature
	Length: Long Illus: Illustration; Table
Subjects:	Mutual funds; Financial performance; Investment companies & advisors; Securities
Abstract:	In the past, a diversified portfolio of small-company stocks has done better than one made up of blue chips. In 1988, the biggest winners stayed away from High Tech stocks, and reaped rewards in health care and entertainment. Several small funds that did that are listed.

copyright © 1996 by UMI Company. All rights reserved.

Record 3

Access No:	00294587 ProQuest Resource/One
Title:	Buying Blue Chips at Bargain Prices
Authors:	Schultz, Ellen
Journal:	Fortune [FOR] ISSN: 0015-8259 Jrnl Group: Business Vol: 118 Iss: 14 Date: Dec 19, 1988 p: 44-46 Type: Interview Length: Medium Illus: Photograph
Names:	Maurice, John
Subjects:	Securities
Abstract:	John Maurice, manager of Putnam's $1.6 billion Growth and Income Fund is interviewed about blue-chip stocks.

copyright © 1996 by UMI Company. All rights reserved.

Record 4

Access No:	00929073 ProQuest Resource/One
Title:	You Can Rely on Stocks but Don't Trust Them Blindly
Authors:	Sivy, Michael
Journal:	Money [MON] ISSN: 0149-4953 Jrnl Group: Business Vol: 20 Iss: 11 Date: Nov 1991 p: 23 Type: Feature Length: Medium Illus: Photograph
Subjects:	Investments; Personal finance; Securities; Portfolio management
Abstract:	An investment strategy for the 1990s should involve keeping at least one-third of one's money in blue chips or top quality mutual funds and rebalancing one's portfolio every six months.
Item Availability:	CD-ROM

copyright © 1996 by UMI Company. All rights reserved.

Record 5

Access No:	00723029 ProQuest Resource/One
Title:	32 Investments to Buy—and Nine to Shun—in '92
Authors:	Willis, Clint
Journal:	Money [MON] ISSN: 0149-4953 Jrnl Group: Business Vol: 20 Iss: 13 Date: 1991 p: 56-60 Type: Feature Length: Long Illus: Illustration
Subjects:	Investments; Securities; Bonds; Business forecasts
Abstracts:	The most promising choices among mutual funds, stocks, income investments, cash and assets are presented. Investments to shun in 1992 are also discussed. Investors should buy small-cap stocks, blue-chips and the funds that hold them—while avoiding long-term bonds.
Item Availability:	CD-ROM

copyright © 1996 by UMI Company. All rights reserved.

Record 6

Access No:	00708681 ProQuest Resource/One
Title:	Bargains in Blue Chips
Authors:	Dingle, Derek T
Journal:	Money [MON] ISSN: 0149-4953 Jrnl Group: Business Vol: 19 Iss: 13 Date: Dec 1990 p: 84-90 Type: Feature Length: Long Illus: Illustration; Photograph; Table
Subjects:	Securities prices; Securities markets; Investments
Abstracts:	The current bear market may offer the best chance of the 1990s to buy high-quality stocks at undervalued prices. Advice is offered on picking blue-chip bargains.

copyright © 1996 by UMI Company. All rights reserved.

Record 7

Access No: 00948721   ProQuest   Resource/One
Title: Blue Chips: For Clues to the Economy's Direction,
                Watch Big Retailers
Authors: Moreau, Dan
Journal: Kiplinger's Personal Finance Mag. [GCHT]   ISSN: 1056-697X
                Jrnl Group: Socio/Environmental; Business   Vol: 45
                Iss: 12   Date: Dec 1991   p: 38   Type: Feature
                Length: Medium   Illus: Photograph; Graph
Subjects: Economic conditions; Retail stores; Securities;
                Financial performance
Abstract: Monitoring the stocks of major retail corporations is a
                good way to tell what turn the economy may take. Brief
                financial performances, including the stock prices of
                Wal-Mart, Sears, JC Penney, and K-Mart retailers,
                are reported.
Item
Availability: CD-ROM

copyright © 1996 by UMI Company. All rights reserved.

Record 8

Access No: 00998527   ProQuest   Resource/One
Title: Three Stocks for Tomorrow Beat Today's Blue Chips
Authors: Willis, Clint; Netzer, Baie
Journal: Money [MON]   ISSN: 0149-4953   Jrnl Group: Business
                Vol: 21   Iss: 2   Date: Feb 1992   p: 47-52
                Type: Feature   Length: Long
                Illus: Illustration; Graph; Table; Photograph
Companies: Reebok International Ltd; Unifi; MGIC Investment Corp;
                IBM Corp; General Motors Corp; Hannaford Brothers Co.
Subjects: Company profiles; Investments; Reorganization
Abstract: Investors won't necessarily make money in the long run
                by loading up on stocks from companies that are reor-
                ganizing and laying off employees, as IBM Corp and General
                Motors Corp are doing now. Three companies that are clear
                winners are Reebok International, Unifi and MGIC
                Investment Corp. The stock pick for Feb 1992 is
                Hannaford Brothers Co.
Item
Availability: CD-ROM

copyright © 1996 by UMI Company. All rights reserved.

NAME _____ DATE _____

Cooking: Entertainment Printout I

Read the printout from the computer search on *Cooking—Entertainment*, found on pages 63–66. Identify the articles you would use to research the following queries. List the articles' titles, authors, and the journals they are found in. Write your answers on the lines provided.

1. How do you organize a cooking club? _____
   _____
   _____

2. Where can you find recipes that you can make ahead of time so that you are not cooking when giving a party? _____
   _____

3. Help! Where can you find recipes that young people will like? _____
   _____
   _____

4. What does it take to be a good party hostess? _____
   _____

5. Where can you find fast and easy recipes? _____
   _____

6. Where can you find information about fruit baskets? _____
   _____

7. Where can you get a recipe for Caesar salad? _____
   _____

PART 5 Reading Computer Printouts **61**

NAME _____   DATE _____

Cooking: Entertainment Printout II

Read the printout from the computer search on *Cooking—Entertainment*, found on pages 63–66. What articles would you use to find information for each of the following research questions? Identify the articles' titles and authors and the journals that they are published in. Write your answers on the lines provided.

1. Where can you find Valentine's Day recipes? _____
   _____

2. What is a brunch? Where are brunch suggestions found? _____
   _____
   _____

3. What are good gifts for cooks? _____
   _____
   _____

4. Where can you find a recipe for cranberry punch? _____
   _____

5. You need a quick weekend meal. What article might give you ideas? _____
   _____

6. Where can you find a recipe for chocolate-almond crunch? _____
   _____

7. Where can you get information on the cost of various culinary gifts? ____
   _____
   _____

62 PART 5 *Reading Computer Printouts*

COMPUTER PRINTOUT: COOKING—ENTERTAINMENT

Record 1

Access No:	01216420 ProQuest Resource/One
Title:	Presents for the Pantry
Authors:	Land, Leslie
Journal:	House & Garden [GHNG] ISSN: 0018-6406 Jrnl Group: Lifestyles Vol: 164 . Iss: 12 Date: Dec 1992 p: 60-63 Type: Features Length: Medium Illus: Photograph
Subjects:	Gifts; Cooking; Gardens & gardening
Abstracts:	No matter how well-stocked one's larder, there is always a spot a cook longs to fill. Gift suggestions for cooks of every taste, including a KitchenAid mixer and fruit baskets, are presented.

copyright © 1996 by UMI Company. All rights reserved.

Record 2

Access No:	00707479 ProQuest Resource/One
Title:	Date with a Dish: Holiday Brunch
Authors:	Lyons, Charlotte
Journal:	Ebony [GEBO] ISSN: 0012-9011 Jrnl Group: Socio/Environmental; Lifestyles Vol: 46 Iss: 2 Date: Dec 1990 p: 108-112 Type: Recipe Length: Long Illus: Photograph
Subjects:	Recipes; Food; Cooking; Entertainment; Christmas
Abstract:	A holiday brunch is a great way to entertain family and friends. A brunch menu and recipes are offered, including holiday chicken patties, oven omelet, eggnog muffins, and hot cranberry punch.

copyright © 1996 by UMI Company. All rights reserved.

© 1997 Good Apple

Record 3

Access No: 00282728   ProQuest   Resource/One
Title: Gifts for Good Cooks: For Holiday Meals and Year-Round
Authors: Kull, Kathie; Hall, Nancy
Journal: Better Homes & Gardens [GBHG]   ISSN: 0006-0151
              Jrnl Group: Lifestyles   Vol: 66   Iss: 12
              Date: Dec 1988   p: 126-128
              Type: General Information   Length: Short
              Illus: Photograph

Subjects: Christmas; Gifts; Cooking

Abstract: Several gift suggestions for people who like to cook
              are provided. Prices are included.

copyright © 1996 by UMI Company. All rights reserved.

Record 4

Access No: 00321796   ProQuest   Resource/One
Title: Tokens of Love
Authors: Anonymous
Journal: Seventeen [GSEV]   ISSN: 0037-301X   Jrnl Group: Lifestyles
              Vol: 48   Iss: 2   Date: Feb 1989   p: 106-107
              Type: General Information   Length: Medium
              Illus: Photograph

Subjects: Holidays & special occasions; Gifts; Recipes; Cooking

Abstract: Recipes for Valentine's Day gifts are offered. Included
              are recipes for chocolate-almond crunch, meringue
              kisses, sweet death cake, chocolate-dipped strawberries,
              and rocky road bites.

copyright © 1996 by UMI Company. All rights reserved.

Record 5

Access No:	00428410 ProQuest Resource/One
Title:	Easy Entertaining
Authors:	Koury, Christine
Journal:	Parents [GPAR] ISSN: 0161-4193 Jrnl Group: Lifestyles Vol: 6 Iss: 8 Date: Aug 1989 Illus: Photograph Type: Recipe Length: Long Illus: Photograph
Subjects:	Food; Cooking; Recipes; Entertainment
Abstract:	A simple menu that can be prepared ahead of time allows the hosts to relax and enjoy their guests. Easy party-planning tips can make these meals a delight to prepare. Recipes are included.

copyright © 1996 by UMI Company. All rights reserved.

Record 6

Access No:	00549906 ProQuest Resource/One
Title:	Gourmet Get-Together
Authors:	Koury, Christine
Journal:	Parents [GPAR] ISSN: 0161-4193 Jrnl Group: Lifestyles Vol: 65 Iss: 3 Date: Mar 1990 p: 153-165 Type: Recipe Length: Long Illus: Photograph
Subjects:	Recipes; Cooking; Food; Entertainment
Abstract:	Information on organizing a gourmet club is presented along with recipes for fried ravioli with sun-dried tomato sauce, Caesar salad, risotto, osso buco, and mocha-brownie semifreddo.

copyright © 1996 by UMI Company. All rights reserved.

Record 7

Access No:	00395567 ProQuest Resource/One
Title:	Why I Haven't Invited Martha Stewart to Dinner
Authors:	Fury, Kathleen
Journal:	Working Woman [WKW] ISSN: 0145-5761 Jrnl Group: Lifestyles; Business Vol: 14 Iss: 6 Date: Jun 1989 p: 152 Type: Commentary Length: Medium Illus: Illustration
Names:	Stewart, Martha
Subjects:	Entertainment; Cooking; Social life & customs
Abstracts:	The author discusses the joys and sorrows of trying to become a proficient hostess. Inspired by dinner-party guru Martha Stewart, she had some interesting experiences entertaining her friends.

copyright © 1996 by UMI Company. All rights reserved.

Record 8

Access No:	00379235 ProQuest Resource/One
Title:	Perfect Meals
Authors:	Turner, Jan
Journal:	Ladies' Home Journal [GLHJ] ISSN: 0023-7124 Jrnl Group: Lifestyles Vol: 106 Iss: 5 Date: May 1989 p: 206-216 Type: Recipe Length: Long Illus: Photograph
Subjects:	Food; Cooking; Entertainment; Recipes
Abstract:	Recipes for delicious meals that can be done quickly and easily for weekday meals or weekend entertaining are given.

copyright © 1996 by UMI Company. All rights reserved.

Name _____   Date _____

Audio Equipment: Automobiles Printout I

Read the computer printout on pages 69–70 for *Audio Equipment—Automobiles*. Write the name of the article and the magazine that it is found in to begin computer searches for each of the following research questions. Use the lines provided for your answers.

1. Where can you find information about car stereo basics?
   _____
   _____

2. What stereo system is available in a Ford Mustang? _____
   _____

3. Where can you find suggestions for the best-sounding systems? _____
   _____

4. What stereo is best for your type of car? _____
   _____

5. Where can you get information on the history of the audio system in Ford Mustangs?
   _____
   _____

6. What journals contain articles on aftermarket car stereos? _____
   _____
   _____

PART 5 Reading Computer Printouts **67**

NAME _____ DATE _____

AUDIO EQUIPMENT: AUTOMOBILES PRINTOUT II

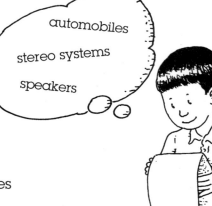

Read the computer printout for *Audio Equipment—Automobiles* on pages 69–70. Identify the articles to use to research the following questions. Include the articles' titles and authors and the journals that the articles are published in. Write your answers on the lines below.

1. How can you reduce the possibility of audio system theft? _____
_____

2. What do the stereo systems of the Ford Mustang and Dodge Intrepid have in common? _____
_____

3. How can you upgrade your stereo system? _____
_____

4. How can you make your car appear as if it has no stereo? _____
_____

5. Where can you see photographs of car stereos? _____
_____

6. Where can you find information on the Lexus GS300's audio system? ____
_____

7. Where can you get information on car stereo speakers? _____
_____

68 PART 5 *Reading Computer Printouts*

COMPUTER PRINTOUT: AUDIO EQUIPMENT—AUTOMOBILES

Record 1

Access No: 01898914   ProQuest   Resource/One

Title: Car stereo update

Authors: Pohlmann, Ken C

Journal: Home Mechanix [GHMX]   ISSN: 8755-0423
               Jrnl Group: Lifestyles   Vol: 90   Iss: 784
               Date: Apr 1994   p: 84-88
               Type: Feature   Length: Long
               Illus: Illustration; Photograph

Subjects: Audio equipment; Loudspeakers; Automobiles

Abstracts: Aftermarket car audio equipment has been popular since
               the 1970s, but car manufacturers are now offering
               systems that rival the aftermarket's best. The basics
               of car stereos and which ones are better for certain
               types of cars are discussed.

Item
Availability: CD-ROM

copyright © 1996 by UMI Company. All rights reserved.

Record 2

Access No: 01556532   ProQuest   Resource/One

Title: Stealth stereo upgrades

Authors: Berger, Ivan

Journal: Home Mechanix [GHMX]   ISSN: 8755-0423
               Jrnl Group: Lifestyles   Vol: 89   Iss: 776
               Date: Jun 1993   p: 42-44
               Type: Feature   Length: Medium   Illus: Photograph

Subjects: Automobile; Theft; Radio equipment; Audio equipment

Abstract: Automobile owners can reduce the risk of theft when
               upgrading a car's sound system by making it appear
               factory-stock. . . .

copyright © 1996 by UMI Company. All rights reserved.

Record 3

Access No:	01922961 ProQuest Resource/One
Title:	Road music
Authors:	Vizard, Frank
Journal:	Popular Mechanics [GPOM] ISSN: 0032-4558 Jrnl Group: Lifestyles; Sci/Tech Vol: 170 Iss: 11 Date: Nov 1993 p: 128-129 Type: Feature Length: Medium Illus: Illustration; Photograph
Subjects:	Audio equipment; Automobiles
Abstract:	Many new cars, including the Ford Mustang, Lexus GS300, and Dodge Intrepid, feature impressive audio systems. The audio systems of the three cars are examined.

Item
Availability: CD-ROM

copyright © 1996 by UMI Company. All rights reserved.

Record 4

Access No:	01874610 ProQuest Resource/One
Title:	Signals: Pony car
Authors:	Pohlman, Ken C
Journal:	Stereo Review [GSTR] ISSN: 0039-1220 Jrnl Group: Lifestyles Vol: 59 Iss: 3 Date: Mar 1994 p: 25 Type: Commentary Length: Medium Illus: Illustration
Subjects:	Automobiles; Audio equipment; Design
Abstract:	In 1994, the Ford Mustang is celebrating its thirtieth birthday with a complete redesign. The car's audio system shows just how far car audio has come over the years.

Item
Availability: CD-ROM

copyright © 1996 by UMI Company. All rights reserved.

Citing Electronic Sources

MLA AND ALA FORMATS

When using periodicals such as magazines and newspapers for a research project, you will need to cite bibliographic and footnote information. There are two recommended formats for citing this information. (Note: examples given are fictitious.)

The *MLA* (Modern Language Association) *Handbook for Writers of Research Papers* suggests the following format.

Bibliography
Weeks, Hillary. "Learning About Computer Research." *Daily News*, 30 Nov. 1997. CD NewsBank from NewsBank, Inc.

Footnote
Hillary Weeks. "Learning About Computer Research." *Daily News*, 30 Nov. 1997: CD NewsBank from NewsBank, Inc.

The *ALA* (American Library Association) *Style Manual for Citing Microform and Nonprint Media* suggests this format.

Bibliography
Weeks, Hillary, "Learning About Computer Research," *Daily News*, Nov. 30, 1997. Located in CD NewsBank [Compact Disc], NewsBank, Inc.

Footnote
Hillary Weeks, "Learning About Computer Research," *Daily News*, Nov. 30, 1997, (Located in CD NewsBank [Compact Disc], NewsBank, Inc.).

Note: Names of newspapers or periodicals, such as *Daily News* or *The Times Journal* should be underlined if typed or shown in italics if computer printed.

NAME _____ DATE _____

MLA (Modern Language Association) Style

You used information from an article in the CD NewsBank database titled "How to Invest Your Allowance" by C.W. Dollar on December 4, 1994, in the newspaper *Your Money*. List below the specific article information requested. Then write bibliography and footnote citations for the article on the lines at the bottom of the page, using the MLA format.

1. Author _____
2. Title _____
3. Newspaper title _____
4. Date _____
5. Database _____

Bibliography

_____
_____
_____
_____
_____

Footnote

_____
_____
_____
_____
_____

PART 6 *Citing Electronic Sources*

NAME _____ DATE _____

ALA (American Library Association) Style

ALA style—American Library Association

You found information in an article titled "Stereo System Upgrades" by Joe Smith in the News Researcher database. The article appeared in the June 1998 issue of the magazine *Home Electronics*. List below the specific article information requested. Then write bibliography and footnote citations for the article on the lines at the bottom of the page, using the ALA format.

1. Author _____
2. Title _____
3. Magazine title _____
4. Date _____
5. Database _____

Bibliography

_____
_____
_____
_____

Footnote

_____
_____
_____
_____

PART 6 Citing Electronic Sources

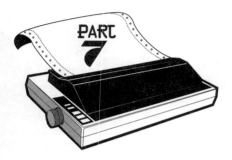

Online: The Internet

EXPLORING THE INTERNET

What is a network? A network is a group of objects or people that work together for a common purpose. The *Internet* is a network of computer networks—computers that are electronically linked around the world to provide a vast array of information.

The Internet system was started by the National Science Foundation when their network of computers became the backbone of the current Internet. Today the Internet is constantly changing and growing as more and more computer networks are added. Lots of resources can be found on this supernetwork, including the card catalogs of many libraries and even library books.

Like computers, libraries exist worldwide. There are different types of libraries, such as public, private, scientific, medical, law, national, and Internet libraries. The Internet can provide access to all of the libraries that are computerized through an online public access catalog. The Internet also allows access to information from universities, government agencies, public organizations and groups, businesses, and individuals. Plan to spend some time exploring this huge resource—the Internet can be a very interesting and rewarding research tool.

HOW DOES THE INTERNET WORK?

Information on the Internet is sent from one computer to another in chunks called *packets*. These packets must be understood by the computer receiving the information, so rules, called *protocols*, have been developed that oversee this process. Packets use the specific code of *TCP/IP* or *transmission control protocol* and *internet protocol*. These codes get the information to its destination. It also codes and decodes the packets.

The networks on the Internet talk with one another through the use of *repeaters, bridges,* and *gateways. Repeaters* keep the traveling information packets going. *Bridges* and *gateways* complete the connection process. A *bridge* connects *local area networks* (or LANs) to other networks in the system. *Gateways* connect different networks.

74   PART 7 Online: The Internet

INTERNET SEARCH TOOLS

In this section actual search tools you may encounter in a computerized library search will be introduced. Information on how to use them will also be provided. Some of these search tools may be available for use on the computers at your school or library. Some work best with older IBM-compatible PCs equipped with monochrome (black and white) monitors that show only text. Others work only with PCs that can show both text and pictures (such as Macintoshes or PCs that use some form of the Windows software). The computer you use may or may not be equipped with the software for one or more of these tools. If you have access to the World Wide Web (WWW), sometimes you can find there no-cost software (called shareware) that will allow you to access a file or you may find links to get to other search tools. (Note: Check with a librarian before attempting to download any shareware to learn if this is allowed. Because some electronic files may be too big for the library's computer to handle, or because of the risk of obtaining unwanted computer viruses, some libraries and schools may not allow this kind of downloading.)

• • • • • • TELNET • • • • • •

Telnet (for *Unix Utility Telephone Network*) was one of the first search tools to be created. Most library computers include Telnet as a tool to search through other libraries' resources, as some information can only be accessed through Telnet. To use Telnet, you need the electronic address of the computer site you wish to search, a *login* and a *password*. A login is a word that identifies you to a remote computer (the computer at another library) so that you can gain access to its files. Most times, the computer you are working from (the *client server*) will make the connection to the computer you wish to search (the *remote* or *host server*). The remote computer will then tell you the needed login and password (if required).

One of the main differences between Telnet and some of the more recently developed search tools is that, with Telnet, once you have connected to a remote computer, the remote computer controls all of the steps in your search for information. Newer search tools allow the computer you are using to guide the search process.

Once you are connected to the remote computer via Telnet, follow the directions that appear on your screen. Address and other information needed to conduct a search are typed in at the prompt (a flashing cursor ■) on the screen, and then the Enter key is hit once. To quit a Telnet search, type **close**, **quit**, **exit**, or **logout** and hit Enter. Look on the computer screen for the exact word (or command) the computer wants you to use to stop a Telnet search. For a listing of sample Telnet sites to explore, see page 80.

PART 7 Online: The Internet **75**

······ Archie and FTP Sites ······

Archie is a computer program that can check computer sites holding data files. These sites are called *FTP*, or *file transfer protocol*, sites. Archie scans what is available on a monthly basis. It even checks to see how files can be transferred. Information in the files can be compressed before being sent. This saves space and time. If information is compressed before the files are sent, the files must be decompressed at the receiving end so that they can be understood.

Archie can be used to search files in three ways: by database file name, by type of file, or by wildcard symbols, such as the * (star or asterisk symbol). Archie cannot retrieve files, it can only tell you where to get them yourself. One way to search for files is to telnet to the Archie server closest to you geographically and login as **Archie**. Type **prog** followed by the keywords you want to search for. Archie will report back with whatever information it finds. In addition, most FTP sites will have a help file, README file, or INDEX file to provide information about the site. These text files can be viewed while connected to an FTP site.

To download files found through Archie, you must use the complete address given by Archie. It's always a good idea to first write addresses down on paper as they must be accurately entered to get you where you want to go! Type the address in and hit Enter to connect to the FTP site. Then respond to the directions on the screen to copy the files to your computer's hard drive. See page 81 for a listing of sample FTP sites to explore with Archie.

······ Gopher, Veronica, and Jughead ······

Gopher is a powerful and easily used search tool. Menus are provided, listing the various search options for you to select from. Gopher's main purpose is to find and browse through files located on computers called Gopher sites or Gopher servers. Gopher is like a book's table of contents. Its sites have links to files at other Gopher sites. These links are valuable because you can quickly connect to another resource without having to look up and type in additional address information. Many libraries, universities, and government agencies have Gopher sites that can be searched. Gopher also searches WAIS (Wide Area Information Server) databases (see p. 77). For a listing of sample Gopher sites to visit, see pages 81–82.

Veronica is a search tool used with Gopher to find a specific topic, document, or keyword. Veronica helps you locate Gopher servers on a specific subject area. Most Gopher sites include Veronica as a menu

76 **PART 7 Online: The Internet**

option. When searching with Veronica, several choices of servers may be given to select from. Always try to use the Veronica server closest to where you live or work. This helps prevent the computer network from bogging down due to too many long-distance searches.

Jughead is a limited version of Veronica. It searches for items by keywords but typically does so only at the site where it is located. This limits the scope of a computer search to include just the resources available locally.

Sometimes when you are using Veronica, Gopher, or Jughead, you may get a message saying that no items were found. When this happens, try again or try first thing in the morning or late in the day. These search tools are heavily used during the daytime hours. This can sometimes cause you to get an incorrect message.

· · · · · · WAIS · · · · · ·

WAIS *(Wide Area Information Server)* is like an index. It is a search tool that looks through the titles and contents of documents on a WAIS server. These documents are available only through this server. WAIS servers can be accessed through a WAIS client, some Gopher sites, the World Wide Web, or by telnetting to a public WAIS client. (A *client* is the computer that requests and accesses information from a server computer.) Gopher and WAIS can work well together in searching the Internet.

Files available on WAIS servers may include texts, bibliographies, library catalogs, Archie databases, and more. WAIS works like Archie and Veronica, except that instead of searching for file names that match your keywords, it searches the actual documents themselves for matches. (Note: Boolean searches are not advised when using WAIS!)

To access a WAIS server, you can use Telnet. Type in **quake.think. com** or **wais.wais.com** and then login as **wais**. The commands to use with each computer system may be different. When in doubt, using a question mark (**?**) at the prompt may provide you with helpful assistance. Access WAIS servers with Gopher on the World Wide Web. Try **gopher://gopher.ub2.lu.se:70/11/allWAIS/experiment/udc/general** or **gopher://gopher.tc.umn.edu:70/11/Libraries** for WAIS servers with research resources. Another way to access WAIS servers from the World Wide Web is to use a search engine such as Excite, Yahoo, Magellan, or Lycos. Type in **gopher WAIS.** Any listings found, along with links to other listings of WAIS servers, will appear on the screen.

PART 7 Online: The Internet **77**

· · · · · · WWW · · · · · ·

World Wide Web *(WWW)*—the easiest-to-use tool for accessing the vast resources on the Internet. The Web is a huge collection of files that are linked together through *hypertext*. Hypertext is text that connects you to another Web page, document, or site when it is selected. On screen, hypertext is usually highlighted in colors that contrast with the color of the main text. To select a hypertext link, use the mouse to move the pointer to the hypertext. An icon, most often in the form of a hand, will appear to "grab" the text. When this icon is visible, click at that point, and you will be electronically linked to the requested document or site. Sometimes all you need to do is to click on the link's name.

To get to a Web site, you use a Web *browser*. A browser is special software that lets you access the Web to find and display a document. Some browsers are text-only browsers and some are text and graphical (or image) browsers. The advantage to using a graphical browser is that you can see pictures included in a document. With text-based browsers you see just the text. Graphical browsers can take more time, though, to process information. This is because images contain lots of data, which requires much more computer memory. The names of some browsers include Netscape Navigator, Mosaic, and Microsoft Internet Explorer. You can explore the Web using older or newer computers, including Windows-equipped IBM-compatible PCs or Macintoshes. The different computer systems require different versions of the browsers, but many manufacturers make browsers for both kinds of systems.

Searches on the Web can be very fast or very slow. Much depends on the number of other computer users who are also trying to access information. Other factors include the distance between you and the server you are using and how memory-intensive the file is that you are trying to obtain. Patience in letting a computer react to your request for information will usually result in your eventually getting what you are searching for. Pressing other keys in the midst of a computer's search or processing of data can confuse the computer and cause you to get strange information or none at all. (Note: Computer servers sometimes go down for repair or maintenance. When this happens, you will get a response on the screen telling you that the server is not responding and to try accessing it later.)

Web site addresses always begin with the prefix **http://**. The letters *http* stand for *Hypertext Transport Protocol*. This is the language that Web browsers use to find linked hypertext documents. Other features

78 *PART 7 Online: The Internet*

that you will see on the browser's main menu screen (the one that appears when you first launch, or start, the program) are the icons at the top: BACK, FORWARD, HOME, RELOAD, IMAGES, OPEN, PRINT, FIND, STOP. If you are in the middle of a search through various links, clicking on BACK will take you to the location just before the one you are currently visiting. If you've gone BACK in your search and then realize you really need information on screens that were ahead of where you are now, clicking on FORWARD will move you up one screen. HOME is the icon to click when you are done searching or to start a new search. RELOAD will reload the file that you've asked the computer to find and show on your screen. This is helpful when, for various reasons, the file does not appear correctly on your screen. To get to a location, or address site, you can click on OPEN, type in the address, and the computer will contact that site to attempt to gain access. The PRINT command will tell your printer to print the document currently showing on the screen. FIND will help you locate a word or term in an opened document. STOP will stop a transfer of data in the midst of a search. This is a useful command if you do not want to continue trying to access a popular search site or if you find that the file you've requested is simply too big. Getting files that contain lots of pictures can require long periods of waiting. Stopping a search and selecting "text-only" in a revised search will help this problem.

The WWW can be used to search for computerized libraries or for actual research information. Resources found in a library some distance from you may still be available to you through interlibrary loan. To learn if there are any online public or school libraries near you, explore the resource listed below. This site maintains a listing of U.S. and international computerized libraries. You can narrow a search by specifying Library Name, City, State, Country, and type of server (such as Gopher, Telnet, or WWW).

St. Joseph's County's List of Public Libraries with Gopher/WWW Servers

http://sjcpl.lib.in.us/homepage/PublicLibraries/ PublicLibraryServers.html

For a list of additional sites able to locate online libraries plus other information resources, see pages 82–84. (Note: Because of the rapidly changing nature of the Web, addresses can go out of date very quickly. If an address has changed and a new one is still available, it will show up on your screen until it is removed from the old Web site. Visit the Simon & Schuster web site at **www.sselem.com** to obtain available *Library Online!* address updates.)

PART 7 Online: The Internet 79

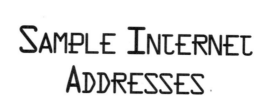

Sample Internet Addresses

······ Sample Telnet Sites ······

Library of Congress Information Systems
locis.loc.gov
Provides access to the Library of Congress holdings, including U.S. government copyright files, federal legislation, organizations, foreign law, Braille, and audio files.

Public-Access Gopher Client
consultant.micro.umn.edu
panda.uiowa.edu
gopher.uiuc.edu
Provides access to a Gopher client for computer users who do not have access through a commercial online service provider (such as America Online, Prodigy, or CompuServe).

World Wide Web Demo
lynx.cc.ukans.edu
login: **www**—Provides access to a text-based Web browser for users not having Web access through their commercial online service providers.

Washington University Libraries
library.wustl.edu
Provides access to U.S. and foreign libraries, medical and law library resources, and a catalog of electronic texts.

Federal Information Exchange
fedix.fie.com
Provides information from various federal agencies, such as the U.S. Department of Agriculture and NASA.

FedWorld
fedworld.doc.gov
Provides access to government databases and other sources of federal information.

NASA Spacelink
spacelink.msfc.nasa.gov
login: **guest**—Provides information about NASA, the shuttle program, and space flight.

University of Michigan Weather Underground
downwind.sprl.umich.edu 3000
Alternate Sites: **rainmaker.wunderground.com**
um-weather.sprl.umich.edu 3000
Provides world weather information, including forecasts, earthquake reports, hurricane advisories, climate data, and more.

• • • • • • SAMPLE FTP/ARCHIE SITES • • • • • •

Gutenberg Project
mrcnext.cso.uiuc.edu (Subdirectory address: **/pub/etest**)
Provides texts of public domain documents including classics, sacred texts, children's books, poetry, and historical documents.

Wiretap Online Library
ftp.spies.com (Subdirectory address: **/library**)
Provides public domain texts of works by Joseph Conrad, Lewis Carroll, Jules Verne, and others, plus various historical and sacred texts.

Smithsonian Institute
photo1.si.edu
Provides photographs of space, art, people, places, nature, technology, and history.

NASA Archives
explorer.arc.nasa.gov (Subdirectory address: **/pub**)
Provides images of space, daily NASA news, mission information, and education resources.

• • • • • • SAMPLE GOPHER SITES • • • • • •

Yale University Library Catalog
yaleinfo.yale.edu
Provides access to library catalogs worldwide for searching or browsing.

Library of Congress Marvel
marvel.loc.gov
Provides access to the Library of Congress card catalog, federal legislation database, Supreme Court rulings, and online exhibits.

Environmental Internet Catalog
infoserver.ciesin.org
Provides weather forecasts, current weather satellite images, movies, and images of natural disasters, and more.

Florida Tech Education Gopher
sci-ed.fit.edu
Provides information on the geography, climate, economy, and political organization of countries and territories listed in the CIA World Fact Book.

Gutenberg Project
gopher.tc.umn.edu
Provides access to public domain documents including classics, sacred texts, children's books, poetry, and historical documents.

Hands-on Science
ralphbunche.rbs.edu
Provides access to scientific discussions, articles, and projects database.

• • • • • • SAMPLE WWW SITES • • • • • •

St. Joseph's County's List of Public Libraries with Gopher/WWW Servers
http://sjcpl.lib.in.us/homepage/PublicLibraries/
PublicLibraryServers.html
Provides listing of and links to online libraries around the world.

The Cyberville Library
http://ncb.gov.sg/cyber/library.html
Provides links to online libraries located throughout the world.

Internet Public Library
http://www.ipl.org/
(or through commercial online service providers:
ipl@umich.edu)
Provides information in science/technology, computers/the Internet, arts/humanities, health/medicine, law/government/ political science, business/economics, social sciences, entertainment/leisure, education, and reference.

© 1997 Good Apple

infoserver.ciesin.org   sci-ed.fit.edu   ralphbunche.rbs.edu   fed1X.fie.com

WWW Virtual Library
http://WWW.W3.org
Provides an indexed listing of and links to various computerized libraries.

Virtual Facts on File
http://www.refdesk.com/facts4.html
Provides encyclopedias, dictionaries, and thesauruses, plus other information on government, law, geography, science, history, population/demographics, world religions, and more.

Planet Earth Virtual Library
http://www.nosc.mil/planet_earth/library.html
Provides information and links to books, libraries, reference materials, encyclopedias, dictionaries, acronyms, time/calendars, scientific constants, periodic tables, weights and measures, weather, Shakespeare, and more.

Webster's Dictionary
http://c.gp.cs.cmu.edu:5103/prog/webster
Provides an online dictionary to use.

Exploratorium
http://www.exploratorium.edu/
Provides science education, virtual field trips, and special science and art exhibits and resources.

Internet Resources for the K–12 Classroom
http://www.ncsa.uiuc.edu/Edu/Classroom/classroom.html
Provides links to physical and social science, math, and astronomy sites plus museums.

The Electronic Zoo
http://netvet.wustl.edu/ssi.htm
Provides pictures and information about a variety of animals.

Dinosaur Hall
http://ucmp1.berkeley.edu/exhibittext/dinosaur.html
Provides pictures and information about dinosaurs.

Rain Forest: White Jag
http://fig.cox.miami.edu/Faculty/NickCarter/whitejag.html
Provides material on rain forests plus links to conservation/ecology sites.

Science Community Action Network
http://edison:scictr.cornell.edu/SCAN/SCAN.html
Provides links to science topics including weather, herbs and spices, critters, orchids, newts, carnivorous plants, math and science gateway, sea animals, NASA and space shuttle information, and more. Cultural links include maps as well as resources on Hispanic, African American, Native American, and Asian heritage. Reference links include the dictionary and Latin grammar.

The White House
http://www.whitehouse/gov/
Provides information on the White House, the executive branch, and the first family plus links to other government agencies and information.

Social Studies School Service Online Resources
http://www.socialstudies.com:80/online.html
Provides resources and links to many museums and more.

History/Social Studies Resources
http://www.acm.cps.msu.edu/~spiveyed/History.html
Provides information and links for topics including flags, maps, government, history, the ancient world, and more.

Civil War Home Page
http://funnelweb.utcc.utk.edu/~hoemann/warweb.html
Provides a listing of resources having anything to do with the Civil War.

Anthropology Home Page
http://www.usc.edu/dept/v-lib/anthropology.html
Provides anthropology, social sciences, museum, and cultural heritage data.

The Gutenberg Project
http://jg.cso.uiuc.edu/pg_home.html
Provides access to various public domain texts.

(Note: Visit **www.sselem.com** to obtain periodic Internet address updates.)

NAME _____   DATE _____

Searching the Internet via Telnet

Review the Telnet locations shown on page 89. Identify the sites that would help you to research the following questions. Write your answers on the lines provided.

1. How can you get a piece of music you wrote copyrighted? _____
   _____
   _____

2. Where might you obtain a book of poetry that is in the public domain? _____
   _____

3. When was the last shuttle launch? _____
   _____

4. Where can you check the forecaster's prediction of a tornado watch for your area?
   _____
   _____

5. Where can you get help translating a menu from the French restaurant? _____
   _____

6. Where can you get information about the latest research on diabetes? _____
   _____
   _____

7. Where could you obtain information on resources for the blind? _____
   _____

PART 7 Online: The Internet   **85**

NAME _____   DATE _____

SEARCHING THE INTERNET VIA GOPHER

Review the Gopher locations shown in the list on page 89. Decide which sites would be good to use to research the following questions. Write your answers on the lines provided.

1. You have learned of a book that will be very helpful in your research. How can you locate and obtain a copy of it? _____
   _____

2. Where can you view a copy of the Declaration of Independence? _____
   _____
   _____

3. Where can you view pictures of damage from the most recent hurricane to hit the Caribbean Islands? _____
   _____

4. Where can you find information on a 1952 Supreme Court ruling? _____
   _____
   _____

5. Where can you find research information on New Zealand mammals? _____
   _____
   _____

6. What was the most recent law enacted by Congress? _____
   _____
   _____

86 PART 7 *Online: The Internet*

NAME _____ DATE _____

SEARCHING THE INTERNET VIA THE WWW I

Review the WWW locations shown on page 90. Find all the sites that would be good for researching the following questions. Rank the sites in order of importance to your search. Write your answers on the lines provided.

1. You are doing a project on Spain. You need information on its capital city, its economy, its flag, and its climate. Where can you find this information? _____
_____
_____

2. Where can you learn what time it is in Greenwich, England? _____
_____

3. Where can you learn more about the members of the first family? _____
_____

4. Where can you find different encyclopedias to provide information on Darwin's Theory of Evolution? _____
_____
_____

5. Where can you gather information about the ocelot's diet? _____
_____
_____

6. How many people live in India and China? _____
_____

PART 7 Online: The Internet **87**

NAME _____ DATE _____

SEARCHING THE INTERNET VIA THE WWW II

Review the WWW locations shown on page 90. Identify all the sites that would provide information for each of the following questions. Rank the sites in order of importance to your search. Write your answers on the lines below.

1. Where can you find information on the culture of Native American peoples? _____
   _____
   _____

2. What sites will tell you more about the tyrannosaur and its habitat? _____
   _____
   _____

3. Where can you get information on the ancient Romans and the places they
   traveled to? _____
   _____
   _____

4. Where can you find a synonym for a word? _____
   _____

5. Where is an online library located that is nearest to you? _____
   _____
   _____
   _____

88 PART 7 *Online: The Internet*

Searching Internet Sites

······ Telnet Sites ······

Library of Congress Information Systems
Accesses Library of Congress holdings, U.S. government copyright files, federal legislation, foreign law, Braille, and audio files.

Washington University Libraries
Accesses U.S., foreign, medical, and law libraries' resources and a catalog of electronic texts.

NASA Spacelink
Accesses NASA, shuttle, and space flight information.

University of Michigan Weather Underground
Provides world weather information: current and long-range forecasts, earthquake reports, hurricane advisories, climate data, and more.

······ Gopher Sites ······

Yale University Library Catalog
Accesses library catalogs worldwide.

Library of Congress Marvel
Accesses the Library of Congress card catalog, federal legislation database, Supreme Court rulings, and online exhibits.

Environmental Internet Catalog
Provides weather forecasts, current weather satellite images, movies, images of natural disasters, and more.

Florida Tech Education Gopher
Provides geography, climate, economy, and political organization information of countries and territories listed in the *CIA World Fact Book*.

Gutenberg Project
Accesses public domain documents including classics, sacred texts, children's books, poetry, and historical documents.

······ Net News Sites ······

Comp	**News**	**Soc**
computers	Internet news	social groups
Misc	**Rec**	**Talk**
many different areas; assorted subjects	recreation (hobbies, arts, and sports)	longer discussions, usually about politics
	Sci	
	science	

PART 7 Online: The Internet

Searching Internet Sites

······ WWW Sites ······

WWW Virtual Library
Provides indexed listing and links to various computerized libraries.

Internet Public Library
Provides information in science/technology, computers/the Internet, arts/humanities, health/medicine, law/government/political science, business/economics, social sciences, entertainment/leisure, education, and reference.

Virtual Facts on File
Provides encyclopedias, dictionaries, and thesauruses, plus information on government, law, geography, science, history, population/demographics, world religions, and more.

Planet Earth Virtual Library
Provides links to books, libraries, reference materials, encyclopedias, dictionaries, acronyms, time/calendars, scientific constants, periodic tables, weights and measures, weather, Shakespeare, and more.

Science Community Action Network
Provides links to science topics, cultural heritage, maps, the dictionary, and Latin grammar.

The Electronic Zoo
Provides pictures and information on many animals.

Dinosaur Hall
Provides pictures and information about dinosaurs.

The White House
Provides links to the White House, executive branch, first family, and other government agencies and information.

History/Social Studies Resources
Provides information and links for topics including flags, maps, government, history, the ancient world, and more.

Anthropology Home Page
Provides anthropology, social sciences, museum, and cultural heritage data.

NAME _____   DATE _____

INTERNET NEWS GROUPS

Information for your research project can also be obtained on the Internet through *news* or *use groups*. News groups may have special names such as *Net News* or *Usenet*. There are so many groups using the Internet that to make it easier to find them, they are usually arranged by broad subject area. Seven of these major groups are listed below. Note that this list identifies groups by a code (an abbreviated form of the group's name). Depending on the software your computer uses to access the Internet, you may find other listings, such as General News, Technology News, Finance, Hardware & Software, Sports, Travel, Entertainment, and Marketplace.

Comp—for groups or subjects that deal with *computers*

News—for a group that discusses *Internet news*

Rec—for *recreation* information: hobbies, the arts, sports

Sci—is the place to explore if *science* is your thing

Talk—if you like to just *talk*, especially about *politics*

Misc—covers *assorted subjects* in many different areas

Soc—provides connections to various *social groups* and *topics*

There are numerous subgroups in each major Internet news group and more are being added every day. Shown below are just a few examples of **misc.** and **rec.** news subgroups to explore.

misc. consumers—consumer products and reviews

misc. invest, funds—bond, stock, and real estate funds

misc. invest, stocks—investing stocks

misc. job, misc—careers

misc. kids, computer—children using computers

misc. writing—talks about writing

rec. aquaria—how to take care of pet fish

rec. arts, comics, market place—comics

rec. arts, Disney—Disney subjects

rec. arts, sf. science—science fiction

rec. arts, startrek—current Star Trek movies and books

rec. arts, tv—history of television

PART 7 Online: The Internet **91**

NAME _____   DATE _____

SEARCHING INTERNET NEWS GROUPS

Review the Net News sites shown in the list on page 89. Decide which sites would be good to use to research the following questions. Write your answers on the lines provided.

1. What does it take to be a medical technician? _____
   _____

2. How should you invest the $1,000 that you just found? _____
   _____

3. Is XYZ soap powder a good product? _____
   _____

4. Does the strange-looking antique bottle that you found have any value? _____
   _____

5. Where can you find a "hot" restaurant in Kentucky? _____
   _____

6. Was Howdy Doody a 1950s television star? _____
   _____

7. Where can you find information about Trekkies? _____
   _____

8. Who is running for public office in your state or community? _____
   _____

Name _____   Date _____

SEARCHING MISC. AND REC. SUBGROUPS

News groups
Misc. subgroups
Rec. subgroups

Read the following research questions. What subgroups on the Internet might provide helpful information? Use the **misc.** and **rec.** subgroups lists on pages 95–96 to locate Internet news subgroups to search for answers to each of the questions below. Write your answers on the lines provided.

1. Where can you find a job description for any retail job? _____
_____

2. Where can you find information about Disney products? _____
_____

3. Where are the best restaurants in Seattle? _____
_____

4. Where can you find information about the Model-T Ford? _____
_____

5. Where can you talk with someone online about science fiction? _____
_____

6. What do you need to know to take care of your pet goldfish? _____
_____

7. Who was Mr. Ed and on what TV program was he featured? _____
_____

8. What are the best stereo components available for the consumer today? _____
_____

PART 7 Online: The Internet   93

NAME _____   DATE _____

IDENTIFYING REC. SUBGROUPS

Translate the following Internet codes into the names of the groups and subgroups on the Internet. Write your answers on the lines provided.

1. rec. arts, tv _____

2. rec. arts, fine _____

3. rec. mag. _____

4. rec. aquaria _____

5. rec. crafts, textiles _____

6. rec. autos _____

7. rec. arts, sf. science _____

8. rec. arts, startrek _____

9. rec. aviation, misc. _____

94   PART 7 *Online: The Internet*

NAME _____   DATE _____

INTERNET NEWS
MISC. AND REC. SUBGROUPS

Some **misc.** subgroups include the following.

1. **misc. consumers**—consumer products and review
2. **misc. education, language, English**—teaching English to non-English speaking people
3. **misc. invest**—general investments
4. **misc. invest, funds**—bond, stock, and real estate funds
5. **misc. invest, stocks**—investing stocks
6. **misc. job, misc.**—careers
7. **misc. kids, computer**—children using computers
8. **misc. taxes**—tax advice and laws
9. **misc. writing**—talks about writing

Some subgroups under **rec.** include the following.

10. **rec. antiques**—antiques
11. **rec. aquaria**—how to take care of pet fish
12. **rec. arts, books**—the publishing industry
13. **rec. arts, comics, market place**—comics
14. **rec. arts, Disney**—Disney subjects
15. **rec. arts, fine**—artists
16. **rec. arts, sf. science**—science fiction
17. **rec. arts, startrek**—current Star Trek movies and books
18. **rec. arts, theater**—about the stage and the theater
19. **rec. arts, tv**—history of television
20. **rec. arts, tv, soaps**—soap operas
21. **rec. audio, car**—car audio systems
22. **rec. autos**—cars, car products, and laws
23. **rec. autos, antique**—cars over 25 years old
24. **rec. aviation, misc.**—subjects about flying
25. **rec. aviation, owning**—owning airplanes
26. **rec. bicycles, misc.**—discussion of bicycling

PART 7 Online: The Internet **95**

27. **rec. birds**—bird watching

28. **rec. boats**—boating

29. **rec. collecting, cards**—collecting sport cards

30. **rec. crafts, textiles**—sewing, weaving

31. **rec. food, recipes**—recipes

32. **rec. food, restaurants**—dining out

33. **rec. food, veg**—vegetables

34. **rec. games, abstract**—strategy of playing games

35. **rec. games, chess**—chess

36. **rec. games, trivia**—discussion of trivia

37. **rec. games, video**—video games

38. **rec. gardens**—gardening

39. **rec. kites**—kite flying

40. **rec. mag.**—the table of contents of magazines and magazine summaries

41. **rec. motorcycles**—motorcycles

42. **rec. music, compose**—musicians

43. **rec. music, makers, guitar**—electric guitar equipment

44. **rec. music, reviews**—reviews of music

45. **rec. outdoors, fishing**—fishing

46. **rec. parks, theme**—entertainment theme parks

47. **rec. pets**—pet care

48. **rec. pets, dogs**—dogs

49. **rec. photo**—photography

50. **rec. puzzles**—puzzles

51. **rec. radio, amateur, misc.**—rules of amateur radio contests

52. **rec. radio, shortwave**—shortwave radio

53. **rec. railroad**—railroad

54. **rec. running**—running

55. **rec. scouting**—worldwide scouting organizations

56. **rec. skate**—skating, ice and roller

57. **rec. sport, baseball**—baseball

58. **rec. sport, football**—football

59. **rec. sport, Olympics**—Olympics